IN SEARCH OF JOHN CHRISTIAN WATSON

Labor's First Prime Minister

Michael Easson

Connor Court Publishing Pty Ltd

Published in 2024 by Connor Court Publishing Pty Ltd.

Copyright © Michael Easson

ALL RIGHTS RESERVED. This book contains material protected under International and Federal Copyright Laws and Treaties. Any unauthorised reprint or use of this material is prohibited. No part of this book may be reproduced or transmitted in any form or by any means, electronic or mechanical, including photocopying, recording, or by any information storage and retrieval system without express written permission from the publisher.

Connor Court Publishing Pty Ltd.
PO Box 7257
Redland Bay QLD 4165
sales@connorcourt.com
www.connorcourt.com

ISBN: 9781923224155

Cover Design by Maria Giordano.

Photo taken from Wikipedia Commons: [Portrait of John Watson] [picture] 1908. 1 photograph : gelatin silver, sepia toned ; 13.9 x 9.2 cm. Part of Members of the Australian Labor Party, Third Commonwealth Parliament, 15 December 1908.

Published in Australia.

*Written in memory of Bede Nairn (1917-2006),
historian of NSW Labor
and for the next generation:
Isabella and Teddy Burke;
Poppy and Oscar Howard*

Official Portrait of Prime Minister Watson, circa, 1904,
National Archives of Australia

Contents

Captions to Photos, Cartoons, and Tables	vii
Author's Note	xi
1. Watson and the Labor Story	1
2. New Zealand-Made; John Christian Watson's First Decades	15
3. Australian-Made; Watson's First 16 Years in Australia	31
4. Labor's Leader in the Commonwealth	43
5. Prime Minister Watson	53
6. Leaving the Parliament for Good	65
7. The Short Triumph of Labourism	75
8. The Unsettled Bargain on National Defence	87
9. Conscription, Expulsion, and Aftermath	95
10. Why the Labor Split Went so Deep and Continued	111
11. Business Life	117
12. Concluding Observations	133
Notes and Abbreviations	143
Watson Bibliography	147
Endnotes	157
Index	189

Captions to Photos, Cartoons, and Tables

Official Portrait of Prime Minister Watson, circa, 1904, National Archives of Australia

Caricature by Hop (Livingstone Hopkins) of Watson, n.d., republished *The Bulletin*, Vol. 84, 18 August 1962, p. 28.

The Little Tin God, *The Bulletin* [Sydney], 12 October 1895, p. 5.

Undated photo of George Thomas Watson. Providence: Professor Ian and Catherine Watson family.

A photo of the early Waipori settlement, n.d., circa 1860s.

A Photo of Mr James Mitchell of Oamaru.

J.C. Watson Sketch. The Eight-Hour Demonstration, *The Daily Telegraph* [Sydney], 3 October 1893, p. 5.

J.C. Watson. Members of the NSW Legislative Assembly, *The Sydney Mail and NSW Advertiser*, 13 April 1895, p. 1.

J.C. Watson, MLA for Young, *The Daily Telegraph*, 15 June 1895, p. 9.

The Unitarian Church in Liverpool Street, Sydney, where Watson was married, n.d., NLA.

The fire damaged Unitarian Church, Liverpool Street, circa 1935, Sydney: City of Sydney Archives.

George Henry Dancey's 1902 sketch for the Melbourne *Punch* was titled 'The real leader of the house: Labour Man Watson – "You lead all right, Edmund – with a little assistance".'

The First Labor MPs elected at the inaugural 1901 election.

Table 1: Federal Elections and Representation in the House, 1901-1910.

Various photos in this portrait of Watson illustrate the story of Watson the busy politician, in the House of Representatives Chamber, reading, speaking to a constituent, and cycling for leisure, *The Australasian* [Melbourne, Victoria], 6 September 1902, p. 564.

John Christian Watson, circa 1902, John Oxley Library, State Library of Queensland; https://hdl.handle.net/10462/deriv/230025.

Lionel Lindsay's Watson, "drawn from life", *The Evening News* [Sydney], 23 April 1904, p. 4.

First Labor Ministry, *Pix*, Vol. 22, No. 12, 19 March 1949, p. 16.

The New Federal Premier [Watson], *Australian Town and Country Journal* [Sydney, NSW], 27 April 1904, p. 24.

Three Men in a Boat. "All Pulling Different Ways", *The Chronicle* [Adelaide], 6 February 1904, p. 32.

Another Official Portrait of the Prime Minister. Source: NAA.

Arthur James Vincent's cartoon on Watson becoming PM: "But we've no experience", *The Bulletin* [Sydney], Vol. 25, 5 May 1904, p. 19.

The Polite Hunters, *Punch* [Melbourne], 19 May 1904, p. 19. The cartoon suggests that divisions and indecisiveness between Reid and Deakin allowed the hare (Watson) to become Prime Minister.

Mr Watson in South Africa, *The Australasian* [Melbourne Victoria], 24 July 1909, p. 222.

The front cover of the Australian National Defence League's *The Call*, No. 3, February 1907.

Labor's NSW How to Vote Leaflet for the Senate in 1917, emphasising the patriotism of the Labor candidates.

Table 2: Federal Elections and Representation Post the ALP Split of 1916/17

Table 3: NSW Elections and Representation Post the ALP Split of 1916/17

Mrs J.C. Watson, *The Daily Telegraph* [Sydney, NSW], 17 October 1925, p. 2.

Wedding photo of Miss Antonia Dowlan. News, *The Sun News Pictorial* [Melbourne, Victoria] 7 October 1925, p. 11.

Watson in NRMA publications wrote numerous articles updating members of campaigns and efforts by his officers to persuade governments to better target road and safety improvements. This one is from 1921.

Old Dog for Hard Road, *Sunday Times* [Sydney, NSW], 15 January 1928, p. 3.

Jim Russell's sketch of Watson, *Smith's Weekly* [Sydney], 23 June 1934, p. 4.

One of many articles in NRMA publications promoting the services offered by the organisation to motorists. This one was published in 1924.

Watson greets Tewksbury at the Opening of the Yellow Cabs Sydney headquarters, *Evening News* [Sydney, NSW], 18 December 1925, p. 1.

The NRMA magazine in November 1941 reports the death of Watson.

Photo of J.C. Watson, n.d., J.C. Watson Papers, MS 451/8/ various photos, NLA.

Author's Note:

When I started this monograph a year ago, my impressions of Watson's role and significance were put to the test. In conversations in the 1980s with labour movement historian Bede Nairn, he told me Watson was the great figure produced by NSW Labor, who shaped the movement more than anyone else.

Watson's legacy is worth knowing and understanding. I now better appreciate Nairn's analysis.

I am grateful to Damian Grace and Catherine Harding for reading an earlier version, correcting mistakes, grammar, and foolish expressions. David Clune made numerous editorial suggestions. Catherine Watson, a direct descendant of one of J.C. Watson's half-brothers, helped me understand the New Zealand period and was vital to drafting of that chapter.

Every mistake, warped conclusion, and infelicitous phrase belongs to me. Such faults, I hope, do not detract from the merit of what follows.

Caricature by "Hop" (Livingstone Hopkins) of Watson, n.d., republished *The Bulletin*, Vol. 84, 18 August 1962, p. 28.

1

WATSON AND THE LABOR STORY

For the 26-years from 1890 to 1916, the Australian Labor Party in NSW and nationally – from creation to flourishing to the catastrophic split over conscription in World War I – was decisively shaped by the personality, style, and ideas of John Christian Watson. During the party's first five formative years, from 1890, Watson was a leading delegate and then President of the Sydney-based Trades and Labour Council (the co-ordinating body of the unions in NSW) and President of the Political Labor League (as the Labor Party was first called). Historian Bede Nairn assessed that NSW Labor's cohesion, direction, and presentation "… was a result above all of the insight, ability, tact and integrity of Watson."[1]

Indeed, there is the strong case that in Labor's first twenty-five years no figure shaped the party more than Watson. He paved the way for his party to win national majority support at elections held in 1910 under his successor Andrew Fisher. Before that there had been two Labor Prime Ministers, and two minority Labor Governments, Watson's for 113 days in 1904 and Fisher's for 201 days from 1908 to 1909.

Watson made his mark as a NSW colonial MP (1894 to 1901), as the first leader of the Federal Parliamentary Labor Party (1901-1907), as Prime Minister in 1904, and as an MP in the first national parliament from 1901 to 1910. As an active participant in party conferences, on the NSW Labor Executive, and on the stump, to the end of 1916 Watson was in the thick of the movement's activities. A typical assessment of Watson was that he "stood for moderation and, undoubtedly, he can claim that he lifted the Labor party high in public favour."[2]

In the 25-years after his expulsion from the party in 1916 over

Their Little Tin God [NSW Premier George Houston Reid kneels before an image of NSW Labor praying for support from the cross benches], *The Bulletin* [Sydney], 12 October 1895, p. 5.

conscription, Watson's political attitudes shifted across the spectrum: ardent hostility to the party which expelled him over conscription in November 1916, to active enthusiasm for the Nationalists under William Morris Hughes to political neutrality in the early to mid-1920s onwards, to open disdain for Stanley Bruce's conservative government in 1929, then support for the UAP in the early 1930s (largely a reaction to NSW Labor demagogue Jack Lang), then again to political neutrality. It is likely he voted in May 1941 for the Labor team led by William McKell at the NSW State elections.

Watson's last quarter of a century was not all about politics; it was mostly business. His most prominent role was as President of the National Roads and Motorists Association (NRMA), 1920-1941. An historian of that organisation noted: "Largely because of J.C. Watson's conviction that the motor vehicle was the transport of the future, the NRMA contributed to all the changes of law and regulation that brought motor vehicles to pre-eminence on NSW roads. From 1925 it brought a competitive edge to the peripheral services available to motorists by providing insurance, introducing the certification of motor mechanics, and outlining the routes for motor tours …"[3]

Throughout his political odyssey and later in his commercial career, Watson retained the aura of the calm, sensible, respectful, and principled man, with a touch of statesmanship, respected across-the-board. Uniquely, of all the senior Labor "rats" who were expelled or left the party over conscription, there was lingering affection for Watson. Upon his death on 18 November 1941, Labor Prime Minister John Curtin in the Labor party room moved a motion of condolence and asked that his Labor colleagues acknowledge and express thanks for Watson's pioneering contributions, including as their first Prime Minister. The Federal Labor Caucus minutes note:

> On the suggestion of Mr Curtin, it was decided:
>> That this Party expresses its deep regret at the death of the Hon. J.C. Watson its first Leader, and the first [Labor] Prime

> Minister; also records its appreciation of his distinguished services to Labor and to Australia and tenders its profound sympathy to his bereaved family.[4]

Similar sentiments were expressed by Curtin in the Australian Parliament. Both Curtin and NSW Labor Premier Bill McKell, along with other political figures Watson knew, were pallbearers at his funeral.

On Watson's career and significance, there is divided opinion. This short work can only touch on some of the key questions which probe his importance in the early development of the Labor Party. Was Watson too addicted to horse-trading with the other parties, seeking concessions when as national Labor Leader he should more aggressively have sought office for Labor in its own right? Was Watson too much in thrall to the dominant statesmen of his time, both in the NSW and Federal parliaments, for the first six years of which, nationally, he was ALP Leader? Did Watson lack self-belief, nimble political instincts, 'grunt' and mongrel, in mastering the parliament and his own party? Was his expulsion in 1916 from Labor avoidable? In the 1916 split, could Watson-the-statesman have tried harder to mollify passions and avert divisions? Was Watson too impressed by Billy Hughes, the Labor Prime Minister from 1915-1916, and Nationalist leader and Prime Minister thereafter to 1923, who had continuously served with Watson in the NSW and Federal parliaments from 1894-1910? Hughes' 'crash or crash through' convictions on conscription together with intemperate attacks on opponents, contributed to the tearing asunder of the House of Labor during the Great War. What is a fair assessment of Watson's legacy? Those are the questions facing his biographers.

There are some myths too that need addressing.

One is that Watson hid his origins. The truth is both yes and no. It was widely known he was born in Valparaiso, Chile, which crops up many times in profiles in the press at the turn of the last century, in *The NSW Encyclopaedia*,[5] and throughout his periods as an MP.

When he died, media reports also referred to this curiosity. Less well known, however, was that he was born of a Chilean-German merchant seaman and a New Zealand woman of Irish Catholic stock, the latter coming to Australia via Tasmania. As the next chapter of this book explains, the origin story is not crystal clear. Records are not extant about the father or what happened to him, though his mother's descendants believe Watson's biological father died while his wife was pregnant; father and son never saw each other. Records were found in Valparaiso by Grassby and Ordonez about the birth and baptism of young Johan Christian Tanck.[6] Much other material that might shed light on his origins are missing. Not much is known as to what happened before New Zealand other than that, within a year of his birth in 1867 mother with child was back, and that the following year, 1869, she married George Thomas Watson, a Northern Irishman of Scots Presbyterian heritage. Young Watson took on his stepfather's surname and he was brought up in a big, poor family in the Otago Province in the South Island of New Zealand. We cannot be certain what Watson knew of the full story.

Long after Watson left political life, there was speculation about where some MPs were born. For example, the American-accented King O'Malley,[7] who once claimed to have been born just across the American border, in Canada. O'Malley was encouraged by Watson to stand in 1901 for a House of Representatives seat in Tasmania.[8] O'Malley continuously held a seat from the Apple Isle from 1901 until defeat in the Australian House of Representatives 1917 election, never to return. Section 41 of the Australian constitution forbids aliens from holding elected office. But I have not seen anything in the contemporary media – when Watson was an MP – which called into question his eligibility. Perhaps no one thought to ask. The better explanation is that no one thought there was anything odd about a person so 'obviously' 'British Australian', as Watson. With O'Malley, in 1896 in South Australia, he successfully sued for libel a published account that said he was an American citizen and fled America over an embezzlement dispute.[9] Despite speculation about his origins, no one pursued the matter seriously.[10] Debates about residence and citizenship only really came to the fore in the 1990s.[11]

Perhaps it is true, as Grassby and Ordonez say, that Watson's only child, Mrs Jacqueline Dunn (1927-2014) née Watson, who was 14-years old when her father died, was told by her mother that her father was born on a ship travelling from Valparaiso to New Zealand.[12] Implicit here is the supposed convention that if a person is born at sea their birth is registered at the next port of call. That would get Watson past any eligibility obstacle. But the evidence is now convincing that he was born in Chile. The High Court of Australia in his time never doubted the eligibility of citizens of the Empire. For various reasons, the law changed in 1999. There was no controversy when Watson was in parliament.

What then of the questions raised above?

The rest of this work shines light on the evidence and assesses what appears right. I put the matter that way because, although some truths are blindingly obvious, some judgement calls are necessary, and some disputable. Some information is missing, such as Watson's own recollections and the records of colleagues and contemporaries. Grassby and Ordonez tell a story from Watson's daughter that an over enthusiastic gardener took clippings and other rubbish and a tin trunk full of papers to the tip.[13] Some material from Watson, however, donated by his widow, was deposited with the National Library of Australia (NLA), but it is not an extensive archive. One document that does survive is Watson's 1914 paper on 'The Labor Movement' in Australia.[14] He spoke on this topic at a meeting of the British Association for the Advancement of Science in July 1914.[15]

How much can we rely on press reports? Few people alive would trust the record of their lives as reported in today's media. Historical figures too are likely to have 'tut tutted' over inaccurate stories, let some 'go through to the keeper', and regretted their unpublished corrections. We can never know the full story of a person whose greatest prominence was 120-years ago. The media are often reliable, too, however. Some articles were clearly inspired by Watson's spruiking and background briefings. We can make informed, educated guesses on what we have. Not everything is lost to the mists of time.

My argument can be briefly sketched. And the chapters that follow add detail and substance to the claims now expressed in summary form.

The first question is whether Watson was pusillanimous in the shifting relationships between Labor and the other parties. Labor held the balance of power in the NSW Parliament and Federally in the entire sixteen years Watson served as MP, from 1894 to 1910. The strategy agreed by Labor representatives in NSW in 1891 was support for the government in exchange for legislative and policy concessions. This achieved piecemeal improvements, gradual change, as outlined herein. This strategy resulted in industrial relations reforms, factory and safety laws, and support for the destitute. Federally, although not by a Labor government, industrial relations law was changed, mostly favourably to Watson's and Labor's ideas concerning compulsory arbitration and conciliation. Watson could say "mission accomplished" after his six years as national Labor leader (to 1907) and leave to his successors the task of building from that base.

Yet, complex questions arise from Watson's achievements as political leader – his view of power, his effectiveness in dealing with circumstances and opportunities, and his pursuit of the Labor agenda. Was Watson intimidated by the so-called great men of his time and unable to boldly conceive a path to dominance for Labor? Certainly, many of the big figures at Federation who were in the parliaments in which he served, including Alfred Deakin, George Houston Reid, and William Lyne respected Watson. The last two became Premiers in the NSW colonial parliament with the support of Labor MPs, including Watson in 1884 and 1899 respectively. Many of those on the conservative side were impressed, one reason Watson was allowed to serve as Prime Minister in 1904. Watson's critics have not seen it this way. Kim E. Beazley, in a critical profile, wrote:

> Was Watson's policy of alliance with Alfred Deakin [the liberal Protectionist Prime Minister, 1903-1904; 1905-1908; 1909-1910] justified? It is very hard to make a case for it. The benefit went one way and not Labor's way. Watson's Government of April-August 1904 was abruptly despatched by Deakin on the issue of preference to unionists [an amendment to legislation on industrial relations law]. Fisher's brief government of 1908-1909 was similarly given no chance to do anything by Deakin.[16]

A similar view, that Watson was 'played with' by Deakin is outlined in a short note by historian Stuart Macintyre. He wrote: "Alfred Deakin, the Liberal leader, cultivated Watson's friendship and support, but Watson was unable, in turn, to bind his colleagues to support the Liberals, so Deakin put Labor in office in 1904 to demonstrate its impotence and then quickly turned it out …"[17] But both these accounts discount significant achievements for Labor in Watson's time.

First, the initial decade of the Commonwealth of Australia was mostly characterised by Liberal-Labor alignment. Progressive reforms were introduced as a result. Second, Labor gained in credibility and respect across the Commonwealth, increasing its votes in elections in 1903 and 1906, under Watson. In 1903 the three parties in the House of Representatives, Protectionists, Free Trade, and Labor, were evenly distributed, giving Watson and Labor a stronger hand. This laid the foundation for Watson's ascension to office in 1904, for Fisher to take office in 1908 and, with momentum and credibility, for Labor and Fisher to win outright in 1910. Third, the adoption of compulsory arbitration legislation was important, even vital, for Labor's institutional base. This was achieved through Lib-Lab co-operation though, ironically, the legislation was only finalised during the time of Reid's prime ministership. Fourth, where the Deakinites and the non-Labor parties refused to tread, Labor saw an opening to champion contrasting policies compared to the non-Labor parties. Age pensions policy was one such area. Sawer notes that before the 1903 election, where Labor's numbers in the House of Representatives caught up with Free Trade and the Protectionist parties, "Labor's initiative was very marked in relation to industrial arbitration, pensions, the note issue, and the Commonwealth Bank. Industrial arbitration in general was a Deakin Protectionist as well as Labor enthusiasm ..."[18] Fifth, the Deakinite liberals split in this period, as did their supporters.

State-action and state-intervention inclined liberals, like H.B. Higgins (who became Attorney-General in Watson's short-lived ministry in 1904), and Isaac Isaacs, made Governor-General in 1931 by Labor Prime Minister James Scullin, were two Deakinite liberals who exemplified this trend. Both Higgins and Isaacs were appointed by Deakin to the High Court in October 1906, Higgins becoming President of the Commonwealth Court of Conciliation and Arbitration in 1907 (from where he delivered the Harvester judgement and defined for generations equity principles in determining 'a fair day's pay' and minimum standards).[19]

Although Reid convinced Deakin about 'fusion' of the non-Labor parties in 1909, this came about largely because Deakin's protectionist vote eroded as he lost MPs to rivals, including Labor, in seats across the country. Deakin was a shrewd and effective political leader for much of his time in the first decade after federation, but he was uncertain of how best to position himself and supporters as Labor became more influential and numerically larger as a party than the MPs he could attract. Sawer suggested:

> Deakin wished to combine the social radicalism of Labor with individualist Liberalism in political organisation under the leadership of cultured middle class professional men such as himself; as he saw it, he wanted to "civilise" Labor; as Labor saw it, he wanted to devitalise Labor.[20]

Those tensions between Labor's aspirations and Deakin's supporters were resolved with the latter finding succour with their erstwhile conservative enemies, the Reidites.

Sawer poses an interesting speculation by saying:

> An amalgamation between Labor and at least the left wing of the Protectionists would have produced a party giving equal emphasis to the "service" and the "social reform" functions of the Commonwealth; such a party would have been richer in administrative talent than either Labor or Protectionist alone, and would probably not have split on the conscription issue ...[21]

But the poor showing of the Protectionists at the 1906 elections meant that previously unthinkable combinations were now in play. The fusion of Deakinite Protectionists and Reid Free Traders/Anti-Socialists in 1909 was indicative of the weakness of the non-Labor parties. Labor's outright victory at the 1910 election came about partly because of the haemorrhaging of some former liberal voters to the Labor camp. Labor was becoming less sectional, a broader party than its base, though strongly aligned with its union origins. Watson facilitated that evolution.

A shaper critique, implied by Beazley's analysis is whether Watson's performance as Labor Leader suggested he lacked conviction? Was this a factor in his resignation as Labor Leader in 1907 and departure from parliament in 1910? A contemporary said of Watson's 'going', that "this voluntary extinction of a shining light is one of the mysteries of contemporary history."[22] The evidence is unclear on the reasons for Watson's departure from political life. He claimed at the time that it was exhaustion and needing a quieter life. He spent most of the year before he left politics, still as the MHR for South Sydney, in South Africa prospecting for gold. This was hard work. Watson had a 'pair' mostly with George H. Reid, the conservative MP, co-founder of the Liberal Party, and Prime Minister of Australia for 10 months and 17 days, after Watson.

When Watson was expelled from the Labor Party in 1916 along with most other major Labor figures of significance in NSW, did he approach the political guillotine recklessly or meekly? Could he have avoided the decision and stayed the hands of those intent on releasing the falling blade? The savagery of the split in Labor ranks over conscription still astonishes. The dynamic, impetuous Hughes was too much for Watson to influence. McMullin captures his character in saying: "… chronic dyspepsia aggravated the mood swings of Hughes's mercurial personality: verve, imagination and charm oscillated with abrasives, tirades and tantrums."[23] Hughes and Watson did not see the pending disaster. In 1916 the Labor Party split over conscription, Watson carried away in the resultant tsunami which devastated so much of what he had laboured for. But it is hard to imagine Watson avoiding the swamping of men and institutions and Labor unity in the aftermath of the first conscription referendum on 28 October 1916.

It only takes two to duel. Each escalation, each denunciation of the other as disloyal to Labor ideals, led to a fierce hardening of enmity. NSW Labor would impose life bans on those MPs who favoured conscription for overseas military service. If ever there was a 'clash' of civilisational attitudes in Australia, it happened in 1916/17, with the unyielding fight over compulsory military service and deployment for all. Watson's role within Labor then and thereafter is poorly explored in the literature. Chapters in this book address this gap in knowledge.

In 1916, both the Federal and NSW Labor governments split and fell, with hitherto veteran Labor leaders, Prime Minister Hughes and Premier Holman, forming 'unity' governments with Labor breakaways and conservative MPs. The history of Labor in Australia, and especially in NSW, in its first 65 years was partly a story of division, bouts of unity, spats and spectacular splits. The big ones were Mt Vesuvius-like in their eruption. Indeed, there is an analogy to be made with Dornbusch's law on financial upheaval: "Crises take longer to arrive than you can possibly imagine, but when they do come, they happen faster than you can possibly imagine" – which gives observers two chances of misreading the phenomena.[24] A similar observation might be made of the sudden, largely unanticipated, bit-by-bit Labor divisions, crises, and schisms in 1916/17, in 1931, and 1954-57.[25]

A fair assessment of Watson's political and Labor legacy requires the perspective yielded through examination of the questions raised earlier. In short, though, this might be said: Watson's approach to labourism, his demonstrable flair in setting out Labor's position on the politics of the day and insistence on the combination of piecemeal and substantive reform – challenges at the heart of politics – decisively influenced the personality of the emergent Labor party. He made the idea of a national Labor government less fearful and less fearsome to his people and the wider public. Weber famously said that "One can say that three pre-eminent qualities are decisive of the politician: passion, a feeling of responsibility, and a sense of proportion."[26] This trilogy applied to Watson. Not that he was perfect. Weber also observes: "This is the decisive psychological quality of the politician: his ability to let realities work upon him with inner concentration and calmness."[27] Weber had in mind the politician focused on practical outcomes. This applies too to Watson, the nimble, conscientious strategist who guided Australian Labor to become a credible, national party capable of governing. The chapter on the brief triumph of labourism elaborates this point. Its justification in this monograph is because Watsonian labourism was a definite species. Understanding Watson's political worldview, how he validated his purpose, how he presented the case for Labor, found its apogee in the first half of the 1910s. The conscription split hid thereafter what could be described as the brief triumph of labourism. That is, Labourism militant, confident of its place and mission.

Nairn's book on the first few decades of NSW Labor is dedicated to John Christian Watson.[28] Nairn argued that by the end of the nineteenth century, "it was clear that the Labor Party could only survive as a powerful force if it adjusted its total activities to the requirements of the electorate."[29] By the early twentieth century, Labor had taken root as a moderate party, but not without tension in its identity. Moderation and compromise became its classic hallmarks and indicative that leaders and supporters saw that Labor objectives could be achieved in constitutional and on-going ways.

It is striking that most contemporary accounts of Watson speak about his strength of character. Nairn's summation of his personality is convincing:

> Watson had ... an effortless ability to relate humanely with practically everyone he knew and an instinctive capacity to instil in others the respect for himself that he had for them. Intelligent and liberal, leadership came naturally to him, the more effective because he could neither patronise nor scorn anyone, reinforced by physical strength, a well-adjusted personality and a down-to-earthness that stopped far short of cynicism.[30]

But criticisms too are shared in the pages that follow.

By the time he died, in 1941, the seed he planted grew to a substantial, if bushfire scarred, spotted gum, with NSW Labor once more under sane leadership, with the party machine mostly harmonious with unions and Macquarie Street. In Canberra, Labor was at the helm at a moment of national crisis, under the leadership of John Curtin. The resilience and approach to government of both Curtin and McKell was unmistakable. It was Watsonian. His example, its remembrance and emulation, was Watson's greatest legacy.

2

New Zealand-Made: John Christian Watson's First Decades

We do not know what John Christian Watson knew of his earliest family history. A person today might be more certain about the evidence than he was or could have been. We do not know what was conveyed to him by Watson's mother. He probably learnt that his natural father died when he was an infant.[1] But we do not know if Watson had any clue about his German origins, which is ironic given his fierce opposition to Prussian militarism in World War I. Watson records many times, on his wedding certificates, in magazine and newspaper profiles, that he was born in Valparaiso, Chile. Neither during nor after Watson left the Federal Parliament in 1910 was there any suggestion of his ineligibility to sit as an MHR. At the time, the Australian Constitution was interpreted as requiring that members of the Federal Parliament be born in the Commonwealth of Australia, the British Empire, or be naturalised Australians.[2] Both origin and eligibility are referred to later in this chapter, the focus of which is to present and examine the evidence on the New Zealand-made Watson's first decades before he left for Australia in 1886.

The cumulative evidence points to this: John Christian Watson's mother was Martha Ellen née Minchin (abt. 1849-1888), daughter of Irish parents William and Ellen Minchin, with siblings William and Sarah. The colony of Victoria's migration records state that members of the Minchin family in 1854 sailed on the emigrant ship 'Star in the East' from Liverpool to Melbourne and then onwards via the steamer passenger ship 'Black Swan II' to Launceston, Tasmania.[3] On that journey, the family consisted of Ellen Minchin 33, William Minchin 12,[4] Sarah 9, and Martha 7. Looking at the ship records, there is more information.[5] The religion for all four is Roman Catholic, they could all read and write, all were born in Dublin, and Ellen was a dressmaker.[6] But why were they in Liverpool? They had escaped. A deadly blight struck the potato crop in eastern Ireland, and from there swept across the country. Poor harvests followed. At least a million people died of starvation and disease. Irish migration to Liverpool, Manchester, Glasgow, and London, swelled the population of those cities in the nineteenth century. Martha was born during the Great Potato Famine (1845-1852), most likely in Ireland. Her family were part of the many Irish that left for survival elsewhere. Between 1845 to 1855, approximately 1.5 million Irish migrated to the United States. Another 600,000 left for England, Canada, and Australasia.[7] Liverpool was the main hub for Irish embarkation to other lands.

The Minchins arrived in Launceston on 7 July 1854 as 'Bounty Regulation Migrants'.[8] Although it varied over time, the Bounty Scheme generally enabled individual Australian colonists to sponsor and employ migrants from the United Kingdom through a 'bounty order'. This allowed the then colonies of New South Wales, Victoria, and Tasmania to boost the numbers and social cohesion of their populations. These colonies desired to attract families rather than single people. When a family arrived, five shillings was paid to the sponsor by the relevant colonial government when each immigrant was approved on disembarkation, the balance after the immigrant lived for 6 months in the colony, though this did not always apply for non-working family members. In 1854, the bounty was £20.00 for each adult, and half that amount for a child under 14 years and older than three, and £5.00 for a child younger than three.[9] William Minchin Snr is recorded as the sponsor, being the "person on whose application [for the family was] sent out" – such application made on 11 February 1854. He is listed as a servant to the Surveyor General of Tasmania,[10] who in 1854 was Robert Power.[11] The ages of the children suggest one certainty and several possibilities concerning William Minchin Snr. That he was already in Tasmania, seeking to be reunited with his family is clear. But when had he arrived? The evidence is inconclusive. One part of the jigsaw includes that a William Minchin, born 1812 aged 40, travelled from Tasmania to Victoria in April 1852 giving his occupation as 'gold seeker'.[12] This is interesting – a possible atavistic link – given Chris Watson's efforts at gold prospecting in 1909 onwards.

The other possibility is the William Minchin who arrived in Tasmania as a convict in 1846, following a trial at the Old Bailey for feloniously assaulting a man on 14 October 1845, "putting him in fear, and taking from his person, and against his will, a watch, value 3l.; and 1 chain, 6d.; his goods,"[13] and conviction on 27 October 1845 with punishment of ten years by transportation to Tasmania. The relevant records say he was born in 1819. But the dates of Mrs Minchin and children coming to Tasmania ten years after his conviction and transportation, assuming the children were all legitimate, do not align. But caution on the accuracy of those records is warranted. As Catherine Watson notes, "… I have noticed with the details of many of my Irish ancestors, that there are issues with the recorded ages on documents, and typically the ages are out by one to two years."[14] The Old Bailey felon, William Minchin departed the UK on 4 March 1846.[15] He is recorded as Roman Catholic, born in county Cork in Ireland, married, with three children.[16] A ticket of leave (which allowed convicts to work for themselves on condition that they remained in a specified area, reported regularly to local authorities, and where possible attended divine worship every Sunday)[17] was granted in December 1850[18] when employed by The Hon. James Lord, a Tasmanian politician and businessman;[19] a conditional pardon was recommended for Minchin in September 1851,[20] and this was granted in January 1853.[21] That timeline means that this Minchin could not be the Minchin seeking gold in Victoria in 1852 (as he would not have been permitted to leave the colony of Tasmania that year), nor, probably, the father of the immigrants arriving in 1854. But it is not possible to entirely rule this out. It is intriguing, that 'both' the William Minchins found in Tasmania at this time were educated. A puzzle arises from the fact that the criminal William Minchin was a gentleman's servant and a French polisher – and could read and write. The Minchin working for the Surveyor General of Tasmania, Mr Power, and the Hon. James Lord could do so too. Is this one and the same person?[22]

So much for Martha's Australian connection, now to her relations in New Zealand. According to her death certificate, Martha arrived in New Zealand around 1862, aged 13.[23] The official New Zealand civil marriage records state that on 19 January 1866 Martha Minchen (sic.) married Johan Christian Tanck in the Registrar's Office, Port Chalmers.[24] Not much is known about him. On the marriage certificate Tanck's profession is listed as Chief Officer of the brig *Julia*, in Port Chalmers,[25] Dunedin's commercial port and township. The vessel had arrived from Talcahuano, Chile, on Christmas Eve 1865.[26] Grassby and Ordonez say that "Johan Cristian Tanck's German family had emigrated to Chile on religio-political grounds from Hanover."[27] It must have been a whirlwind romance between Minchin and Tanck, unless they knew each other from earlier stopovers in port.

A newspaper report refers to a civil wedding by special licence at Port Chalmers between "John Christy Tarick, Esq., of Valparaiso, to Miss Martha Ellen Skinner, the youngest daughter of James Skinner, Dunedin."[28] Catherine Watson comments: "This newspaper clipping was interesting, as it was one of two newspaper clippings in Martha's [hymnary]."[29] Martha's wedding clipping was glued to the front of the book, the other, about the diamond wedding anniversary of G.T. Watson's parents was loose – which makes sense as the latter happened after Martha had died.[30]

Nairn says the witnesses to the Tanck-Minchin marriage were "James and Ellen Martha Skinner."[31] Nairn's 1978 genealogical note is the first reference to Tanck in the accounts of J.C. Watson's life. There was a sizable German-origin population in Chile, Grassby and Ordonez saying: "The Tancks opened an import/export business with the Herbst clan and became well established and settled ..."[32] They say Watson's biological father was born in Chile,[33] never joined the family business and, instead, made his career in seafaring. Nairn says the newly married couple departed Port Chalmers for Guam on 2 February 1866.[34]

With his marriage on 30 October 1925 to Antonia Mary Gladys Dowlan, J.C. Watson records his mother's name as Martha Skinner.[35] The most convincing explanation is that Martha was known as both Skinner and Minchin. Her wedding certificate to George Watson says Minchin, but she was also known as Skinner. Indeed, on the birth certificates of her children, her maiden name is sometimes Skinner, sometimes Minchin.[36] The evidence points to Ellen Minchin having married or eloped with a James Skinner and moved to New Zealand.

As for J.C. Watson's birth, there is little room for doubt. Though, again, there are some surprising inconsistencies in the available evidence. Nairn says: "It may be true that he was born on 9 April 1867 at Valparaiso, or on a ship between there and New Zealand."[37] Watson's granddaughter, Mrs Jacqueline, "Jacqui" Dunn,[38] née Watson, once declared: "My mother was always adamant that my [grand] father was born at sea, in international waters."[39] In a book published in 1918 on figures of note in the British Empire, the assertion is made: "J.C. Watson was born in 1867, actually on an emigrant ship, which was conveying his parents to the colony."[40] But Grassby's and Ordonez's research clinches the case for Chilean birth, on the balance of probability.

Referring to J.C. Watson as "the forgotten man with the invisible childhood";[41] those authors through their research were determined to make amends for his unknown or opaque childhood. They say: "On arrival [that is, on returning to Chile from New Zealand] at Valparaiso, Tanck registered his marriage with the Matriz Catholic Church."[42] They point out, however, that no birth certificate for J.C. Tanck the younger – or of the elder, the father – has been found: "In all likelihood, it was destroyed in the fire at the Catholic Church of Matriz, where all such records were kept. However, a record of the birth is held by the Mormon Church at Santiago, which has acquired many Chilean records."[43] Frustratingly, Grassby and Ordonez do not say what, exactly, they saw of the Church of Latter-Day Saints' records. But they do conclusively refer to records that show that Tanck's vessel, *La Joven Julia*,[44] was docked in Valparaiso port on 9 April 1867, the generally accepted date of JCW's birth.[45]

Interestingly, there is no mention in the New Zealand official records of the relevant period of a Tanck birth on land or on the way over the oceans. Hearsay was that if a child was born in international waters, the birth was registered at the next port of call. Hence, Mrs Dunn's mother's supposed insistence on the birth having been on the high seas. But place of birth is a red herring.

Section 44 (i) of the Australian Constitution disqualifies any person who "is under any acknowledgment of allegiance, obedience, or adherence to a foreign power, or is a subject or a citizen or entitled to the rights or privileges of a subject or a citizen of a foreign power." Those words, since Watson's time, and subsequent to enactment of citizenship laws of some countries which require active endeavours and fulfilling of defined procedures to renounce and relinquish citizenship, led in the last 25 years to a more strict interpretation by the High Court of Australia, such that any citizenship of a foreign power, including dual citizenship, means that a person cannot take a seat in the House of Representatives or the Senate, even if 'elected'. For the first time, in 1999 the High Court of Australia, sitting as the Court of Disputed Returns, ruled that Senator-elect Hill of Queensland was ineligible due to her joint citizenship of Australia and the United Kingdom.[46] This was arguably new law or, finally, an accurate enforcement of S.44(i). No longer could British subjects or citizens of the Commonwealth be eligible to hold elected office in Australia, Australian citizens only, and no person holding joint citizenship, is eligible. Because this debate occurred more than 80 years after Watson left the Federal Parliament, it is nonsense to say J.C. Watson

Undated photo of George Thomas Watson. Providence: Professor Ian and Catherine Watson family. Catherine Watson to Michael Easson [email], 10 February 2024.

contrived to hide his Chilean origins.⁴⁷ He did not. There was no need to. The eligibility law had not yet been recast or redefined.

Nairn says that J.C. Watson:

> ... went to school at Cave Valley,⁴⁸ leaving at 10 to become a nipper on railway construction works. After helping on his father's farm, at 13 he was apprenticed as a compositor to the *North Otago Times*. In 1882, described as a "lanky, alert-looking, youth", he was with the *Oamaru Mail* and in 1886 was a member of the local typographers' union and of the New Zealand Land League. Losing his job in 1886, he migrated to Sydney.⁴⁹

A profile on Watson, published in New Zealand when he became Australian Prime Minister, says:

> As he was not born with a silver spoon in his mouth, he went to work at an early age – 10 years – and began by assisting the navvies on one of Sir Julius Vogel's railway works, his wages being five shillings a day – high wages for a boy of 10. The hard, healthy work in the bracing climate of New Zealand gave him a wiry frame and robust health that have stood him in good stead under the strain of politics, and after rising so far in the railway world as to drive a "dobbin," he left the navvying, and was apprenticed, at 13 years of age, as a compositor.⁵⁰

Interestingly, in the early 1860s gold was discovered around the Waipori River, Otago, and the surrounding wild tussock country was pock-marked by mining tenements. On their way came gold diggers, shopkeepers, publicans, bullock drivers, and George Thomas Watson, seeking his fortune. JCW's stepfather, however, failed in this endeavour. He moved to Weston, then Oamaru, finding work as a labourer.

As a 10 years old nipper, young Watson worked with his father, making tea for the men, doing odd jobs, and looking after the tools.⁵¹ When he was apprenticed to the *Oamaru Mail*, Grassby and Ordonez say that "he received his first introduction to the world of

A photo of the early Waipori settlement, n.d., circa 1860s, Waipori Gold website, *Waipori history – Waipori Gold*, accessed 3 January 2023.

politics and trade union activity. The foreman of the day in the print shop, a James Mitchell … selected Watson as the brightest apprentice of them all."[52]

Watson leaving school to work so young, in 1877, suggests the family were in penurious circumstances. They were: In January 1876, George Thomas Watson was declared bankrupt,[53] and a meeting of creditors was held in early February that year.[54] In December 1878, an advertisement appeared for G. Watson about an auction that month for "Section 9, Block I, Weston Township with well-built five-roomed house thereon."[55] It did not sell. The family were struggling financially.

It is likely the family were near destitute, close-knit, and desperate for sustainable employment and regular income for the chief bread winner. Bread and dripping might have been one aspect of home life, low rations another. But it was not all grim. Aged 17, Watson in 1884 is described as the Honorary Secretary of the Weston Cricket

Club.⁵⁶ He seems to have regularly played.⁵⁷ Another newspaper report in December 1884, refers to J.C. Watson as a member of the *Oamaru Mail* team versus the *Timaru Herald*'s in a friendly rifle shooting competition.⁵⁸ In scavenging for status, sporting prowess was always one of his strengths, as were his written and verbal skills.

Bringing home income was key. Watson's apprenticeship as a compositor meant he was no longer as much of, or at all, a financial burden, even if apprentices' wages were not grand. His mother, as discovered below, was glad he was learning a trade. The *Oamaru Mail* in 1884 had a circulation of around 1400 subscribers. In 1884, Watson was one of the newspaper's agents for subscription orders in Weston. His name appeared numerous times in that capacity in the newspaper from 1884-1887.⁵⁹ Mrs Watson appeared as an agent for the *Oamaru Mail* starting from early 1887, after her son departed New Zealand for Sydney, to early 1888 (her death).⁶⁰

According to the *Cyclopedia of New Zealand* in 1905:

> The first edition of the 'Mail' is published daily at 3 p.m. and is timed for despatch by various trains. The journal is a four-page paper of twenty-eight columns and has a daily circulation of 2,100 copies throughout the North Otago and South Canterbury districts. ... A water motor, supplied from the corporation water works, and a gas engine drive the plant, which consists of a two-feeder double royal Wharfdale machine, two Platen machines, three linotypes, and other up-to-date appliances, besides an ancient machine on which, it is said, the first issue of the 'Melbourne Age' was printed and also the first issue of the 'Otago Daily Times'. Of course, this 'old identity' is superannuated and is in fact little better than a museum specimen.⁶¹

Linotype equipment was introduced in 1899,⁶² well after Watson arrived in Australia. The antique equipment described in 1905 was almost certainly what Watson worked on.

Despite frustrations about training limitations, canvassed below, Watson learnt his trade and completed his 'articles'. He was mentored not only about how to set type, but also about how to put together and write a story. His 'printing chapel' experiences, in New Zealand and Australia, educated him. Pakeha print culture activity in the Otago region, in Oamaru, Windsor, and beyond, was represented by lively, small newspapers which were the primary tool of communication among communities:

> From the price of grain, literary jottings, and serialized fiction to inflammatory attacks on government policies, newspapers were the spaces where local and regional identities were forged, and where print culture was clearly viewed as a practical tool in an emerging colonial society.[63]

Working where he did, with interesting and opinionated people, the young Watson thrived.

John La Nauze, biographer of Deakin, noted the benefits of this education at the *Oamaru Mail*:

> Watson's experience as a compositor is reflected in some interesting ways in his correspondence. His punctuation was meticulous, and he used the appropriate conventions to indicate italics and diphthongs (as when he wrote of 'an appeal to Caesar', with the 'close up' sign for 'ae'). Moreover, he knew when to use a semi-colon. Mr M.H. Ellis, whose written reflections of Watson have been most helpful, recalls 'the strong hands and spatulate fingers of the old-time hand compositor'.[64]

In Oamaru, after he lost his job in May 1886, Watson posted an advertisement to sell a boat, 14ft long, sails, mast, oars, complete,[65] suggesting that by then he had decided to seek his fortune in Sydney and was selling up, in preparation.

Away from home, in financial and employment difficulties in Sydney, Watson was to learn, alone, that his mother had died on 30 January 1888. He still had family in New Zealand, the people he grew up with, but his future success all depended on him.

What was Watson like as a young man? Some glimpses are suggested in newspaper remembrances. After Watson became Australian Prime Minister on 27 April 1904, a friend or acquaintance posted this memory to a New Zealand newspaper:

> The first time I met him was in … 1880. At that time, I was employed in the *Oamaru Mail* office by the Honourable George Jones. Watson came on the scene as an apprentice to the composing room and was subjected to a good deal of chaff on account of his country ways, and, according to his own statement he had just finished "a job picking spuds". He was never afraid of criticism and would, without hesitation, talk to the whole of the compositors about any boyish pranks we had or were about to indulge in. His father was at that time working in a stone quarry at the small town of Weston, and I remember distinctly hearing his mother remark to a neighbour: that "Chris is all right, he is learning a trade." Part of Chris Watson's duties consisted in lighting the editor's fire and he was in the habit of opening up the exchanges and reading them with great interest. On more than one occasion I have heard the foreman, 'Jimmy' Mitchell, remark in a sarcastic way, "Now then Mr Watson, when you have finished writing that leading article, we will have your services in the composing room." Jimmy Mitchell is still employed in the *Oamaru Mail* office …[66]

This suggests Mitchell was a formative influence, a point soon to be returned to.

Watson ascension to the Australian Prime ministership sparked other memories too. A notable sketch appeared in 1904 by "An Old Friend" in the *Catholic Press*, which was widely syndicated in other Australian newspapers. This piece began:

> I first met John Christian Watson at Oamaru, New Zealand, when he was a boy of 13 or 14. [i.e., 1880/81] His father was dead, and he lived with his mother and stepfather and three sisters in a little wooden house near the town.
>
> It is said they were small farmers. They might have been years before, but at this time they had no land. The stepfather was the principal breadwinner, and young Jack [Chris] was helping to keep the little home together. He had been

working since he was 10. They were all deeply attached to one another. The mother was a fine, simple, lovable woman, and her children adored her.⁶⁷

The article went on:

> Jack [Chris] came on to George Jones *Oamaru Mail* as a printer's 'devil'. There I first met him. He was a good, earnest lad, willing to turn his hand to anything. The 'Mail' is a small country newspaper, and on country papers the 'devil' is at the beck and call of everyone in the office. He has to clean the ink-rollers, wash down the machine, sweep up the compositors' room and the machine room, turn the handle of the printing machines, and deliver the papers to the subscribers.
>
> He worked about fourteen hours a day for 8s a week. All the time he was picking up as much as he could of the trade. Young Watson performed all these duties for over twelve months, and then he got a better opportunity to learn the regular trade of a printer.⁶⁸

This assertion begs the question of what better opportunity was there? Surely the writer is mistaken, unless he is thinking that Watson's moving to Australia, finding compositor jobs in Sydney, was what he had in mind. The article ended:

> He has always kept close in memory the old home in New Zealand. His mother is dead, and his stepfather is now blind. I think his three sisters are married. He and Mrs. Watson visited them not long since, and Mrs. [Ada] Watson told me the parting was heartbreaking, they are all so attached to one another.⁶⁹

Watson's life in New Zealand spurred an interest in working out how best to change the world. His departure coincided with New Zealand's 'long depression' in the 1880s and his loss of his employment in 1886.⁷⁰ For Watson, clearer ideas and determination about what to do lay ahead, in Australia.

Arriving in Auckland in late December 1929,⁷¹ Watson visited Oamaru in January 1930.⁷² A report noted that when revisiting his boyhood, workplace in Oamaru,

Watson looked in at the newspaper office there, where 'Watson' is scrawled on the old frame where he snatched type half a century ago. One ancient who set type beside him was there to give him the hand of welcome. His old boss (James Mitchell, the doyen of M.L. [i.e., Maori Land] journalists) died a few hours before Watson's arrival at Oamaru. The apprentice of 50 years back was one of the pallbearers at the funeral.[73]

At the time, Jimmy Mitchell was "perhaps the oldest working journalist in New Zealand".[74]

A Photo of Mr James Mitchell of Oamaru, from the collection of the North Otago Early Settlers' Association Portrait Collection; photo taken by D.H. Gilmour, Mahan Studios, 1920s, Forrester Gallery, Waitaki Museum and Archive, New Zealand.

working since he was 10. They were all deeply attached to one another. The mother was a fine, simple, lovable woman, and her children adored her.⁶⁷

The article went on:

> Jack [Chris] came on to George Jones *Oamaru Mail* as a printer's 'devil'. There I first met him. He was a good, earnest lad, willing to turn his hand to anything. The 'Mail' is a small country newspaper, and on country papers the 'devil' is at the beck and call of everyone in the office. He has to clean the ink-rollers, wash down the machine, sweep up the compositors' room and the machine room, turn the handle of the printing machines, and deliver the papers to the subscribers.
>
> He worked about fourteen hours a day for 8s a week. All the time he was picking up as much as he could of the trade. Young Watson performed all these duties for over twelve months, and then he got a better opportunity to learn the regular trade of a printer.⁶⁸

This assertion begs the question of what better opportunity was there? Surely the writer is mistaken, unless he is thinking that Watson's moving to Australia, finding compositor jobs in Sydney, was what he had in mind. The article ended:

> He has always kept close in memory the old home in New Zealand. His mother is dead, and his stepfather is now blind. I think his three sisters are married. He and Mrs. Watson visited them not long since, and Mrs. [Ada] Watson told me the parting was heartbreaking, they are all so attached to one another.⁶⁹

Watson's life in New Zealand spurred an interest in working out how best to change the world. His departure coincided with New Zealand's 'long depression' in the 1880s and his loss of his employment in 1886.⁷⁰ For Watson, clearer ideas and determination about what to do lay ahead, in Australia.

Arriving in Auckland in late December 1929,⁷¹ Watson visited Oamaru in January 1930.⁷² A report noted that when revisiting his boyhood, workplace in Oamaru,

Watson looked in at the newspaper office there, where 'Watson' is scrawled on the old frame where he snatched type half a century ago. One ancient who set type beside him was there to give him the hand of welcome. His old boss (James Mitchell, the doyen of M.L. [i.e., Maori Land] journalists) died a few hours before Watson's arrival at Oamaru. The apprentice of 50 years back was one of the pallbearers at the funeral.[73]

At the time, Jimmy Mitchell was "perhaps the oldest working journalist in New Zealand".[74]

A Photo of Mr James Mitchell of Oamaru, from the collection of the North Otago Early Settlers' Association Portrait Collection; photo taken by D.H. Gilmour, Mahan Studios, 1920s, Forrester Gallery, Waitaki Museum and Archive, New Zealand.

To return to a point raised in the first chapter herein, Watson's origin story is clouded. Even an admiring portrait of Watson written by his apparent confidant H.M. Ellis remarked:

> His father, George Thomas Watson, is generally described as a sailor. Chris Watson was a little off-hand about it when I asked him; but no meaning could be written into this since he was a stickler for the old fashioned convention that an Australian's home was his castle and his private life private.[75]

Perhaps Watson did not want any attention given to his mother and her familial circumstances. Being part of the Watson clan, the family who made him feel as one, was enough.

We are all products of our environment. Those words turn from cliché to potent and poignant force in considering Watson's life. Treating citizens with dignity, ensuring that the catastrophically injured are not left to charity, enabling effective and enforceable health and safety regulations, and old aged pensions – these are what J.C. Watson fought for. His New Zealand life shaped him profoundly. Like nearly all the Labor pioneers, Watson knew what it was to go hungry. What happens to a person in their formative years always influences their future selves, never more so than for those drawn to public service via the vocation of politics.

3

AUSTRALIAN-MADE:
WATSON'S FIRST 16 YEARS IN AUSTRALIA

It is remarkable that within eight-years of descending from the gangway to shore in Sydney, Watson went from unemployment, penury and hunger, to odd jobs, including as a stablehand at the Governor's residence, to employment as a compositor on Sydney newspapers, to activity and leadership of the union movement as President of the Trades and Labor Council, President of the NSW Political Labor League, as the conciliator-pacifier-unifier at Labor party conferences. That prepared him to seek and win election as a Labor MLA for a country seat, Young, in the NSW parliament. That was the broad trajectory of Watson's life, 1886 to 1894: hard scrabble and tremendous success.

He served in the NSW colonial parliament to Federation in 1901, and then as an elected Federal MHR to 1910. In 16 of his first 24 years in his adopted country he was a respected parliamentarian, and from 1901 a national figure.

By the time he arrived in the colony of NSW, the post-European settlement version of the country, 'Settler Australia',[1] was almost a hundred years old, supplanting the Aboriginal peoples who had lived on the continent for upwards of 65,000 years.[2] Sydney's population grew from 16,000 in 1833 to 378,000 in 1891.[3] The Australian-born Europeans, the sons and daughters of the emancipated and free settlers, and a steady stream of migrants from the British Isles, including Ireland, as well as those from across the Tasman Sea, performed wonders in the Australian colonies, the new, emerging nation. Belich, interestingly, comments about cross-Tasman identities:

> How long it takes to make an 'Australian' or a 'New Zealander' is a vexed question; and the possibility of an Aus-

tralasian collective identity – vague and loose, but real – complicates the picture further. Some people, in contrast to the colonising crusaders, did not see the two shores of the Tasman world as significantly different places. Their movements were more akin to internal than external migration.[4]

Perhaps 17% of Victoria's migrants in the 1880s, for example, were from the Land of the Long White Cloud.[5]

In 1886 Watson got low financially, and pluckily tackled any work that came along. A job in Government House stables came up, under Governor Carrington. Ellis recalls:

> I happened to mention Lord Carrington to him, and he said pensively: "He was a good little man. I worked in his garden a bit. One day he spoke to me as I was going off and asked me about myself. He gave me sixpence for a beer and I spent it on a book."[6]

But the young printer got tired of the long and irregular hours unavoidable in his billet. He was next employed at lumping timber, and then got work at his old trade on Sydney's protectionist organ *The Globe*, which subsequently became *The Star*.

Australians mostly thought they were building a better world. A few sang praises for the possibility of an Antipodean Utopia, but the adrenaline rush which led to such ambition, mingled with disil-lusion, was mostly in check. The most notable exception, leaving aside some of the small socialist sects, was William Lane's[7] decision to lead in 1893 a convoy of the scorned, defeated unionists and their families across the Pacific and through the Argentine to Paraguay, the ill-fated 'New Australia' colony, about which more, later.

Sensible people like Watson were skeptical of the concept of utopias, building something divorced from traditions and the messy cut-and-thrust, turmoil, and dynamism of the society in which they lived and breathed. Making the place better was the hard-boring work they set out to achieve. What evolved in the land – the victories, defeats and prosaic campaigns of the unions included – was not to be dismissed. A series of struggles, industrial and societal, forced

MR. J. C. WATSON
(President of the Trades and Labor Council).

J.C. Watson Sketch. The Eight-Hour Demonstration,
The Daily Telegraph [Sydney], 3 October 1893, p. 5.

change, as celebrated in the phrase 'eight hours labour, eight hours recreation, eight hours rest'. This slogan was deployed by stonemasons in Melbourne who, on 21 April 1856, won an industry-wide agreement to establish the Eight Hour Day. The ambition behind that success was a rallying-call for all other workers. The achievement symbolised workers' determination to take control over the time of their lives to balance their lives equitably between work, rest, and play. As Kimber and Love say: "It was an assertion that they were not simply 'operatives' in a labour market, but also family members and citizens in what they hoped could become a civilised community."⁸

On 14 April 1891, at the Catholic Young Mens' Association Hall Watson and John West spoke at the inaugural meeting of the Labor Electoral League in West Sydney.⁹ In August 1892, Watson was elected President of the Trades and Labour Council.¹⁰ For the next few years, he presided over conferences of the Labor Party which defined and refined the 'pledge'.¹¹ Black accused Watson of having stacked the Special Labor Conference held on 9 November 1893 which canvassed the wording of the pledge. Perhaps Watson had a hand in the gathering of delegates and the numbers. Arguably, only he could pull off a consensus position. Fitzhardinge argues: "Benign, courteous, and imperturbable, Watson was the only man equally at home on both sides of the movement, in which his dual chairmanship gave him a key position."¹² In 1894, the resolution at the Labor Conference was:

> (a) That a Parliamentary Labor Party to be of any weight, must give a solid vote in the House on all questions affecting the Labor Platform, the fate of the Ministry, or calculated to establish a monopoly or confer further privileges on the already privileged classes, as they arise; and
>
> (b) That accordingly, every candidate who runs in the Labor interest should be required to pledge himself not only to the fighting platform and the Labor platform but also to vote on every occasion specified in Clause (a), as a majority of the Parliamentary Labor Party may in caucus decide.¹³

Hagan and Turner argue that the party's adoption of the pledge and the Caucus system eventually allowed it to exercise a discipline over its members that was greater than its rivals. "The ultimate penalties for breaking the pledge were loss of endorsement and expulsion from the party — and as the Labor Party gained in repute, so it became more difficult for candidates who were not endorsed and official candidates to win votes in competition with those who were."¹⁴ Yet some, including Joseph Cook, briefly Labor's Leader in NSW, left after the 1884 pledge – and because he felt more comfortable as a Free Trade conservative, aligning with Reid.

Patient, incremental improvements – factory legislation, safety nets – the relentless pursuit of progress with fairness was the labour movement's aim. And in its unfolding was created a freer society, alive, fascinating, passionate, and stable. A unique quality of life began to flourish. Not that this was perfect; far from that. The vagaries of the market, the absence of pensions, workers' compensation insurance, unemployment benefits, adequate housing, sanitation, medical and health support, made life grim for many. Australians sometimes fretted about themselves, their identity sourced from other lands in a newly forged environment. Australia's youthful grace was of the unbound and the uncouth, direct, open, with irreverent "Jack is as good as his master" confidence. Because in this period Australians felt so far away, all alone in the world, such sentiments encouraged a 'do or die' determination, a belief that men and women here had to stick together. Pride and cringe, nationalism and Empire-loyalty, mingled in complementary and contradictory tension. Most Australian colonials saw themselves as part of the British Empire, but free to make their way in the world, to seek a better place rather than merely mimicking the original. Australia was an on-going adventure. This, then, was the spectacle: Australia, from the late nineteenth century onwards attracted attention as a possible model, a social laboratory. Australians were a people who danced the dance of life more boisterously than most others. But the tipping-over gales of economic shocks were never far from view, as the early 1890s were to reveal.

In the NSW elections of 1891 in the two-member electorate of Young, Labor won both seats. But in the ensuing parliament both MPs rejected 'the pledge', refusing to be bound by any Labor Caucus decision on platform issues. When he was President of the Trades and Labour Council of NSW, Watson had some familiarity with Labor politics in Young. At a meeting of the Executive of the Council on 13 April 1893, Council received a request from the Young Branch of the General Labourers' Union asking for printed material explaining the Labor cause; and they returned thanks for what was sent.[15] In July 1893, the Young District Trades Hall Council wrote to the Council stating that in view of "the inevitable and desperate struggle looming in the near future when the great mass of Australian workmen must resist capitalistic terrorism… [there is the need] to effect an early and lasting settlement of industrial disputes…"[16] The Young Council wrote to their 'brothers' in Sydney urging the intensification of Labor political organisation. Watson saw his chance after the two Labor members for Young quit the party. Watson made himself available for preselection, hoping that miners, rail workers, and agricultural workers were a solid base for Labor. On 14 January 1894, Watson thanked Mr. W.A. Hourn, secretary to the Young branch of the Labor Electoral League, for the members' endorsement. After expressing gratitude, Watson wrote:

> Dear Mr. Hourn, — I desire through you to tender to the Labour League for having, by so decisive a majority, selected me to run in the interest of labour at the next election. It is impossible for me to express adequately my recognition of the compliment tendered me— rendered more valuable by the fact that I went amongst you almost a stranger; but I am sure you will have no cause to regret your choice.
>
> … I am sure there is little need to remind the energetic workers connected with the Young branch that they must not rest content with having selected a man to run. Many people are opponents of ours only because they do not understand fully our aims and aspirations, and no opportunity should be lost by members, either individually or collectively, of sweeping away the mists of prejudice which prevent a clear conception of the many reforms for which the Labour Party are striving. Speaking now, as President of the Central Committee of the Labour League I may say there will be but a very few seats for which Labour candidates will not be run at the next election, and while we can-

not expect to win all, there is little doubt that the old political 'hacks' will find themselves hopelessly in the minority when the battle is over ...[17]

Watson stood for Labor at the general elections on 17 July 1894, winning a plurality of the vote (it was the 'first past the vote' voting system in that election.) The two sitting, ex-Labor members ran against each other as Protectionist candidates, scoring a bit over a quarter of the vote each, but losing to each other and to Watson in what was now a single-seat electorate of Young.[18]

Admiringly, an article in the Catholic press remarked: "Watson has had no University training. It is questionable if he went to a primary school more than two or three years. He had no 'pull', no social influences whatever to lift him up."[19] Yet he was a success. He had learnt so much along the way. The article went on: "If you wanted him on off hours, you did not look for him in a favourite public-house. You knew you would find him either in his home or in a library. In the debates at Labor gatherings, he soon displayed superior knowledge and intelligence, supported by a stern character and a genial and attractive manner."[20] A similar observation was made in a profile in the Melbourne *Leader* newspaper:

> ... he early evinced an omnivorous taste for reading. No book was either too tough or too thin for his literary digestion, and consequently he acquired a knowledge of things encyclopaedic in scope... the material was there... destined to distinguish him above his fellows when he came to bestir himself in trades unionism and politics.[21]

The author of that article noted that Watson in 1894:

> ... went to the newspaper manager and asked if, in the event of failure to win a seat, he could return to his work, the newspaper manager said No: he should either stay at his work or leave the office altogether. This only fired Watson's spirit of independence. He resigned his position, stood for Young, and was elected.[22]

It was a 'do or die' decision.

J.C. Watson, Member of the NSW Legislative Assembly, *The Sydney Mail and NSW Advertiser*, 13 April 1895, p. 1.

J.C. Watson, MLA for Young, *The Daily Telegraph*, 15 June 1895, p. 9.

Labor did well in rural areas partly, as Watson said, because: "... the Labor Party at once associated itself with the demand for cheap land, and thus secured considerable support in the country districts."[23] He retained the seat of Young throughout his membership of the New South Wales Assembly, on the last occasion in 1898 beating by nearly two to one Mr. R.E. O'Connor.[24] In the NSW Parliament, Watson particularly devoted his energies to land legislation, and in 1895 argued for the replacement of the system of condition purchase by deferred payments, with the perpetual leasing system combined with the principle of periodic appraisal for rent. The reform was a partial homage to Henry George land policy with Watsonian characteristics. The purpose of the new law was to checkmate the land speculators, the spurious settlers, and what in New South Wales is known as the 'peacock' – the man first in to pick the eyes out of the land and first out at a profit.

Reading some of what Watson stood for, it is shocking to see his mainstream but terrible racism. He was 'of his time' as the saying goes, but on this matter stridently and fiercely so.[25] At the central body of unions in the colony, the NSW Trades and Labour Council, at different times calls were made for a tax on Chinese in the colony, the banning of Chinese-made furniture, and the labelling of Chinese-manufactured goods so that purchasers might be beware of their origin, and the banning of Chinese migration.

When Watson became the member for Young in 1894, his existing prejudices might have been reinforced, as the town was notorious for anti-Chinese riots during a Gold Rush. A mob of 2,000-3,000 men had rallied and attacked Chinese miners at Lambing Flat in June 1861.[26] Lambing Flat became known as Young, officially, from 1869, named after Sir John Young (1807-1876), the then Governor.

In 1901, Watson raised the spectre of a mixed-race Australia, warning of "racial contamination."[27] In his 1914 essay on 'The Labor Movement', Watson acknowledged how the policy of 'White Australia' might seem strange to people in other countries: "To those unacquainted with local conditions the cry for a 'White Australia' may seem somewhat hysterical, but there is no question upon which Laborites are more united and determined."[28] He references the riots in Victoria between Europeans and the Chinese during the 1850s onwards Gold Rush: "It will be seen that the original objection to coloured immigrants was a purely economic one, but as experience was gained of their habits and standards of living it was realised that they could not be absorbed into the community without risk of serious deterioration socially."[29] He adds a corollary to the need to protect the Australian way of life by insisting: "Australians are realising that to maintain their ideals they must fill their waste spaces and prepare for effective defence."[30]

In February 1897 speeches by W.J. Ferguson,[31] Labor MLA for Sturt, and Watson expressed reservations about Federation: "…their differences were upon the method of it."[32] The Labor view was to oppose equal representation of the States in the parliament. NSW Laborites were worried about undemocratic features of the draft constitution. But once the decision was made, the next task – for Watson and for Labor – was to make the most of new opportunities.

Before discussing Watson's national role, a brief note on religious affiliation is worth noting. Roy Williams in his account of the spiritual convictions of Australian Prime Ministers describes Watson as a "fellow traveller", someone who "admired Christianity and followed its basic non-theological precepts."[33] But he is not sure beyond that: "On matters of religion, Watson was unique", with a German-Lutheran father, an Irish-Catholic mother, brought up in New Zealand by a Scottish born Presbyterian stepfather who married his mother. At one point, he sought instruction in the Catholic faith, but did not complete the conversion. That was after his marriage on 30 October 1925 to Antonia Mary Gladys Dowlan, who was of Catholic background. Although he was twice married in the Unitarian Church in Liverpool Street, Sydney, first in 1889[34] to English-born Ada Jane Low, dressmaker, who died on 19 April 1921, "[t]here is no solid evidence that Watson ever worshipped regularly at the Unitarian

The Unitarian Church in Liverpool Street, Sydney, where Watson was married, n.d., NLA.

The fire damaged Unitarian Church, Liverpool Street, circa 1935, Sydney: City of Sydney Archives.

Church."³⁵ The minister who married him, the Rev. George Walters, in May 1904 gave a pulpit estimate of the then new Federal Prime Minister:

> I venture to say that the present Premier, Mr. J.C. Watson, is one of the cleanest, straightest, and most honourable of those who have, or have had, the destinies of the Commonwealth in their care and keeping. When, in this church, 14 years ago, I married him to his partner in life, I hardly anticipated that he would become Premier of a united Australia; but, from that day to this, in humble or exalted position, John Christian Watson has been a true man, whom we may respect and admire.³⁶

As a fire destroyed the church in Liverpool Street and most of its records, and Watson's documents are scant on the point of his religious beliefs, it is not possible to appraise how strong his adherence to Unitarianism might have been. In December 1904 the Church afforded him an opportunity to speak on 'Christian Socialism',³⁷ which is discussed in Chapter 7.

4

LABOR'S LEADER IN THE COMMONWEALTH

The first Federal Parliamentary Labor Caucus consisted of eighteen men. At that first meeting, Watson recalled that Josiah Thomas, "a Cornishman and a wonderfully able debater, particularly around economics, though a free-trader, moved to my great surprise, that I should be elected leader of the Caucus."[1] Charles MacDonald, MHR for Kennedy in Queensland, proposed Andrew Fisher, "but the majority voted for me, possibly because I had the advantage of knowing quite a number of them before the elections."[2]

La Nauze, in his biography of Deakin, said:

> Unlike the stately Barton and the formidably comic Reid, men whose names were familiar throughout the continent, [Watson] was a leader for whom, at that time, any other member of his party might have been substituted without causing the slightest surprise to members or to the public.[3]

That was so, given that outside the state from which they were elected, "…all the Labor men were unknown and none had national name-recognition."[4] La Nauze offers a provocative perspective: "It was not long before it was evident that the first decision of the Labor Party, its choice of a leader, provided a powerful argument in support of its official belief in the virtue of collective wisdom."[5]

Watson attracted the eye of a few perceptive chroniclers and analysts of his political emergence, seemingly without trace, from NSW onto the national stage. One liberal-inclined writer-sage commented:

> It is a curious circumstance… that although he had necessarily to go the full lengths of advanced and ever advancing Liberalism, there was a point where Liberalism had to halt while Laborism stumbled on with a vague and somewhat bewildered mission to digest and assimilate the uncooked Utopianism of more or less unscientific and emotionally enthusiastic Socialistic writers. As is usual with immature

politicians, imagination often outpaced practicability, and failure has been recorded for many a Labor party experiment, prematurely attempted and only elementally developed. In such cases the Laborites have invariably had to seek shelter in the Liberal camp and patiently await the advance of the main army towards the end to be achieved.[6]

The notion that Laborites were a kind of species of practical Liberals was condescending yet suggested an open mind about the pretensions of this still newly minted party. While Labor was a distinct minority in the House of Representatives, as in the first parliament from 1901-1903, "Deakin himself appeared happier with Labor rather than Free Trade support."[7]

A sketch of the state of politics in October 1902 bemoaned "only one man in the House has had a policy and a determination to achieve it, and that is Mr Watson, and he has had all along the line. The nominal leaders of the House have vied with each other in their efforts to soothe and serve him."[8]

George Henry Dancey's 1902 sketch for the Melbourne *Punch* was titled 'The real leader of the house: Labour Man Watson – "You lead all right, Edmund – with a little assistance"'. Barton, Australia's first PM, is taken by the scruff of the neck and propelled forward by Watson. National Portrait Gallery, Canberra.

The First Labor MPs elected at the inaugural 1901 election:

Back Row: Charles McDonald (MP, Herbert, Queensland); Senator George Pearce (WA); Josiah Thomas (MP, Barrier, NSW); Jim Page (MP, Maranoa, Queensland); James Fowler (MP, Perth, WA); Senator John Barrett (Victoria); Senator David O'Keefe (Tasmania)

Middle Row: David Watkins (MP, Newcastle, NSW); Thomas Brown (MP, Canobolas, NSW); King O'Malley (MP, Tasmania); Hugh Mahon (MP, Coolgardie, WA); Senator William Higgs (Queensland); Andrew Fisher (MP, Wide Bay, Queensland); Senator Hugh de Largie (WA); Frederick Bamford (MP, Herbert, Queensland)

Front Row: William Spence (Darling, NSW); Senator Anderson Dawson (Queensland); Senator Gregor McGregor (South Australia); Chris Watson (MP, Bland, NSW); Senator James Stewart (Queensland), Lee Batchelor (MP, South Australia), James Ronald (MP, Southern Melbourne, Victoria)

Kneeling: Frank Tudor (MP, Yarra, Victoria); Billy Hughes (MP, West Sydney, NSW).

Creator: Barroni & Co.; Trove PIC/5876 LOC B19, NLA.

Under Watson's leadership after 1901, Labor increased its vote and representation in the Federal parliament, as Table 1 shows.

Table 1: Federal Elections and Representation in the House, 1901-1910[9]

Party	1901 Votes[i] %[ii]	1901 Seats	1903 Votes %	1903 Seats	1906 Votes %	1906 Seats	1910 Votes %	1910 Seats
Free Trade/ Anti-Socialists[iii]	30.03	28	34.37	25	38.17	27		
Protectionists	36.75	31	29.70	26	16.44	16		
Liberal Party[iv]							45.09	31
Independent Protectionists				0	4.84	4		
Labor	15.76	14	30.95	23	36.64	26	49.97	43
Western Australian Party				0	2.33	2		
Independents	1.66	2	4.49	0	1.58	0	4.94	2
Revenue Tariff Party	0	0	0.49	1				
Others	15.80	0						

Notes:

i) At the 1901 election, voting was determined by the individual states and voting eligibility varied between states. Thereafter, for all elections to 1919, the voting system was based on the adult franchise at 21 years; single member districts; first past the post (plurality) voting. In 1919, optional preferential voting was introduced for Australian elections.

ii) Percentages based on the rate of voting in contested seats. In 1901, six seats, all held by Protectionists, were elected unopposed. In 1903, 17 electorates were uncontested, 11 Protectionist, four Free Trade, and two Labor. Whereas in 1906, seven members of the House of Representatives were elected unopposed – three Anti-Socialist, three Labor, and one Protectionist. In 1910, four were uncontested: two each to Labor and Liberal.

iii) Free Trade became the Anti-Socialist Party in 1906.

iv) In 1910, the Anti-Socialists and Protectionists merged to form the Liberal Party, the "fusion party".

ILLUSTRATED INTERVIEWS

FEDERAL LABOUR LEADER MR. J. C. WATSON, M.H.R.

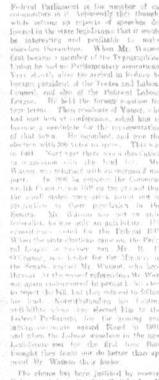

ILLUSTRATED INTERVIEWS: MR. J. C. WATSON, M.H.R., FEDERAL LABOUR LEADER.

Various photos in this portrait of Watson illustrate the story of Watson the busy politician, in the House of Representatives Chamber, reading, speaking to a constituent, and cycling for leisure, *The Australasian* [Melbourne, Victoria], 6 September 1902, p. 564.

With the principle of compulsory arbitration – and legislation to that effect being drafted for the Federal parliament – Watson eschewed any reflex instinct to favour strikers. Speaking of striking coal miners at collieries in the Hunter Valley, in early 1904 Watson told the *Newcastle Morning Herald* that, "In his opinion, they had acted very unwisely … they should have resumed work and have proceeded by the proper channel … Their indiscreet course of action had not shaken his faith in the principle of compulsory arbitration or of the Act."[10] On the question of arbitration, Watson remarked that some employers resented the restrictions on their 'freedom' to do as they pleased. On the other hand, "some extreme Socialists would say that it is deservedly meeting the fate of all merely ameliorative measures …"[11] Watson argued that the cost to the community and the benefits overall, including for individuals and families had to be weighed: "… where they have been loyal to the law their victories have been secured at infinitely less cost to themselves and with a corresponding saving to the community as a whole."[12] One important impact of compulsory arbitration was "… the benefits conferred upon the large aggregate of women and other workers who were practically incapable of organisation …"[13]

Federally, what was required of the Labor leader was a capacity to reconcile the divergent views of the representatives of the several States. The fiscal issue was the most prominent iceberg on the waters. Mindful of how the non-Labor parties in NSW divided and split the NSW Labor MLAs on this matter, Watson strove above all to attain and then maintain Labor unity. The lack of splits, and the cohesion of the Federal Labor Party under his leadership, was one indication that Labor's Leader was a harmonious force. Politics, in Crick's formulation, is a branch of ethics done in public, "amid the open canvassing of rival interests,"[14] in which experience plays a central role, where there is recognition that "there are differing interests and values to be conciliated in societies and that public procedures for reaching acceptable compromises can be institutionalized."[15]

Watson insisted that as much as protection and free trade were

John Christian Watson, circa 1902, John Oxley Library, State Library of Queensland; https://hdl.handle.net/10462/deriv/230025.

matters of principle, they were also circumstances of expediency. A profile on the Labor Leader noted: "Mr. Watson's attitude on the incidence of the tariff has been conspicuous much more by the spirit of compromise than by any marked or enlightened display of leadership."[16] This character sketch declared:

> Mr. Watson is not very distinguishable from the practical, active Liberal. He has none of the intemperate views of the agitator variety of Labor representative and holds strongly to the sound opinion that to go too fast is a twin evil to go-

ing too slow. The set-back following upon a hasty advance is too prone to leave things worse and more retrograded than before. In appearance he is a good looking, thoroughly alive, and polished young politician. He is no great orator, but always assured of a good hearing because he speaks with authority and always has something pertinent to say. In the House he is well esteemed, and is likely, from the common sense of his nature, to rather lessen than broaden the now narrow gap that exists between legitimate Liberalism and incautious, impetuous Laborism. There is accordingly no exciting or picturesque element in the history of the thirty-five years of his life. He has few inclinations outside his politics, rowing being the only active form of recreation in which he indulges. At the same time, he has no impossible ideals, a steady consistent evolutionary progress being his theory of the proper course of political improvements.[17]

This article appraised and praised:

…if statesmanship means the possession of political principles which may be applied to practical politics, of patriotism which has stood untainted amidst popular outcries, of leadership which has triumphed all along the line in Parliament and in the country, of readiness and power in debate, the capacity to hold a House and command serious attention, then, assuredly, young Watson is more than a politician. On all questions that arise in Parliament he has displayed wide and accurate knowledge, an unsleeping vigilance, and a criticism which has not only been destructive but helpful. Sitting amongst his followers in his corner of the House, there is no one who can ignore his force and personality. Watson by his leadership has won for the Labor party more than the sympathy of the working men. It has to-day the respect of the thoughtful of all classes, and it looks as if it is going to have their support in a measure which a few years ago had not been anticipated by anyone.[18]

An important task of a political party's leader is to maintain the respect of colleagues, to keep everyone united as much as possible, and to recruit where possible new talent. Alec Poynton MHR joining the ALP in 1904 under Watson was one example of the latter. Poynton, notwithstanding labour movement sympathies and history, won election as a Free Trader in 1901 from South Australia. His admiration for Watson was a reason he joined the ALP.[19]

Lionel Lindsay's Watson, "drawn from life", *The Evening News* [Sydney], 23 April 1904, p. 4.

5

Prime Minister Watson

Reporting to Whitehall, in April 1904 the Governor-General Lord Northcote noted that on an amendment moved by the Labor Party to include Commonwealth and State public servants under the purview of the proposed Conciliation and Arbitration Bill, the Deakin Ministry lost by nine votes in the House.[1] In a coded message Northcote also wrote speculating that "Mr Watson...hopes that, if the Arbitration Bill can be disposed of, his party and Mr Deakin's may form a close alliance." Northcote went on: "Mr Deakin is, probably, nearer to the Labor Party than to the regular Opposition on fiscal questions; & will certainly wish to give the new Ministry a fair trial."[2]

HISTORIC GROUP of first Commonwealth Labor Ministry, 1904. Standing: E. L. Batchelor, A. Dawson, A. Fisher, H. Mahon, W. M Hughes (grasping chair). Sitting: G. McGregor, J. C. Watson, H. B. Higgins.

First Labor Ministry, *Pix*, Vol. 22, No. 12, 19 March 1949, p. 16.

The New Federal Premier [Watson], *Australian Town and Country Journal* [Sydney, NSW], 27 April 1904, p. 24.

From the moment he assumed office as Prime Minister, Watson bore the demeanour of a statesman. Hughes in *Crusts and Crusades* describes the new PM:

> Mr Watson, the new Prime Minister entered the room and seated himself at the head of the table. All eyes were riveted on him; he was worth going miles to see. He had dressed for the part his Vandyke beard was exquisitely groomed; his abundant brown hair smoothly brushed. His raiment was a veritable poem – a superb morning coat and vest, set off by dark striped trousers, beautifully creased and shyly revealing the kind of socks that young men dream about; and shoes to match. He was the perfect picture of the statesman, the leader ...[3]

Yet, as Holman remarked: "The path of the Watson Government was... from the beginning strewed with thorns."[4] This was because the new government lacked a majority and was at the mercy of the other parties.

The *Hansard* for the House of Representatives, 2nd Parliament, 1st Session, on 27 April 1904, records Watson rising to his feet:

> His Excellency was good enough to approve of the names submitted for the administration of the various Departments, and I will read from to-day's *Gazette* the list of the members of the new Administration, with the office allotted to each: -
>
>> The Honourable John Christian Watson, Treasurer and Prime Minister;
>>
>> The Honourable William Morris Hughes, Minister of State for External Affairs;
>>
>> The Honourable Henry Bournes Higgins, K.C., Attorney-General;
>>
>> The Honourable Egerton Lee Batchelor, Minister of State for Home Affairs;
>>
>> The Honourable Andrew Fisher, Minister of State for Trade and Customs;

>The Honourable Anderson Dawson, Minister of State for Defence;
>
>The Honourable Hugh Mahon, Postmaster General.
>
>In addition to the names mentioned, the Honourable Gregor McGregor has been called to the Executive Council as Vice President of that body. I wish to add, on behalf of my colleagues and of those members with whom I have been so nearly associated, that we deeply deplore the fact that, owing to the severe illness of [Sir Charles Kingston] the Right Honourable member for Adelaide – an illness in which I know he has the sympathy of every member of the House – we have been deprived, unfortunately for Australia as well as for ourselves, of the ripe experience, statesmanship, and patriotism which he might otherwise have brought to the councils of the Ministry.

This reference to the radical liberal and former Premier of South Australia indicated Watson's innate caution and pursuit of respectability. In choosing Higgins and attempting to procure the services of Kingston, Watson projected Labor to the public and the parliament as worthy of government: a combination of experience and raw enthusiasm, ministerial novices plus seasoned parliamentarians. It was also a nod to the idea of small 'l' liberal and ALP alignment in the interest of effectively governing the Commonwealth.

The 1903 elections resulted in a parliament about which Alfred Deakin's famous line about 'three elevens', was coined. Speaking at a meeting of the Australian Natives Association, Deakin asked: "What kind of a game of cricket could you have … if you had three elevens in the field instead of two, and one sometimes played on one side, sometimes on the other, and sometimes for itself!"[5] The parties commanded 26, 25, and 23 seats each, with one independent. The 'three elevens' was a cricket analogy, as if the natural order was to have two teams only competing. One of the consequences of three elevens was a revolving door of Prime Ministers. From 1903 to 1906 the PMs were – Barton (NSW), Protectionist (who resigned in fa-

Three Men in a Boat. "All Pulling Different Ways", *The Chronicle* [Adelaide], 6 February 1904, p. 32.

vour of Deakin shortly before the 1903 election); Deakin (Victoria), Protectionist; Watson (NSW), Labor; Reid (NSW), Anti-Socialist, previously Free Trade; and Deakin again.

Another Official Portrait of the Prime Minister. Source: NAA.

On the same day as Watson announced to the House the formation of his ministry, Deakin responded:

> It is a happy augury that, however much we may differ on points of policy, we are able to avoid those interchanges of personal combat which, though made on behalf of a party,

must appear in some measure due to personal ambitions. I take advantage of the opportunity extended to me to sincerely congratulate the Prime Minister upon the success which has attended his efforts to form an Administration. The task which the Ministry is about to essay is one of which he has exhibited a proper appreciation based upon his present knowledge, but his appreciation will be greater three weeks hence, and still greater within three months.

Which might have inadvertently conveyed another augury: that the Watson ministry would be given three months to govern.

Deakin went on to tantalisingly offer the possibility of alliance with the new Prime Minister:

I feel confident that the same tact and moderation which characterised the Prime Minister while he led his party on the opposite benches will be continued, that he will lay before this Chamber no chimerical or impossible schemes of work, but that he will invite us to join him in carrying out the policies on which we were both returned, and thus enable us to fulfil our duties to the people of this country.

To which Mr Watson was recorded in *Hansard* as saying: "Hear, hear." Mr Reid, the Leader of the Opposition, remarked:

The late Prime Minister [Mr Deakin], upon a somewhat interesting occasion some months ago, described the parliamentary situation as one in which three elevens were playing a game of cricket. Well, as matters have turned out, my honourable friend the Prime Minister has courageously engaged to play any other twenty-two, and that is the contest to which he is committed.

The convivial politeness of the occasion was broken by those words of Reid:

Whilst personally I have real esteem for the new Ministry, both collectively and individually, and whilst I can never forget the generous support extended to me in New South Wales by two of its leading members [Watson and Hughes, when Reid was Premier of NSW, 1894-1899], we all know that in the performance of our public duties we have to keep ourselves as free as possible from personal considerations.

In other words, he would oppose where necessary and support when deserved the actions of the new government. Reid announced:

> The main question, however, under our system of government, is not the pious, well-meaning desires of persons who happen to be in positions of power, but whether they have been placed in their positions by the evolution of the will of the people of Australia as reflected by their representatives. …a majority of the people of Australia did not wish for, and did not vote for, the establishment of an Administration such as is the present one. I cannot by any polite phrases disguise the seriousness of the existing position.

The Parliament then adjourned, giving the new ministry three weeks to acclimatise to their unexpected portfolios. The *Daily Telegraph* reporter opined: "The success of [Watson's] leadership has been a considerable surprise to those who knew the man and the party he had behind him, for it cannot be gainsaid that the majority are extremists in their opinions and would have been more extreme upon their plastic Government of Sir Edmund Barton if they had been controlled by an undoubtedly "sane" man at their head."[6]

The title of McMullin's book on Watson's government, *So Monstrous A Travesty* (2004) conveys some of the horror of conservatives to the ascension to office of a Labor Prime Minister and a Labor Government. Rapturous greetings of Watson and his team at public meetings and in the Labor press, stood in sharp contrast. Besides Hughes, Watson was closest to Batchelor. Of Adelaide-born Egerton Lee "Batch" Batchelor (1865-1911),[7] Watson said he was "one of the sanest and most gracious colleagues one ever had."[8] A pupil-teacher then member of the Amalgamated Engineers' Society, Batch was a South Australian state MP, 1893-1901, and, with permission of his Labor colleagues, Minister for Education in the free-trade Holder state government[9] from 1899-1901. He resigned from state parliament to win election from South Australia to the first federal parliament at the same time as Watson. In the latter's 1904 ministry, Watson notes he "was the only member of our first Federal Caucus who had any effective training in Cabinet life."[10] One of Watson's colleagues in the Ministry, Hugh Mahon, suggested: "If Mr Watson had had his way probably Sir George Turner [Treasurer under Barton and Deakin] and Sir Frederick Holder [the former South Australian Premier and MHR] would have been invited to join him."[11] But Watson sensed that would be a step too far for his Labor colleagues.

Arthur James Vincent's cartoon on Watson becoming PM: "But we've no experience", *The Bulletin* [Sydney], Vol. 25, 5 May 1904, p. 19.

The Polite Hunters, *Punch* [Melbourne], 19 May 1904, p. 19. The cartoon suggests that divisions and indecisiveness between Reid and Deakin allowed the hare (Watson) to become Prime Minister.

But what did his government achieve? Beazley's barbed criticism about Watson's alleged timidity must be considered. Little by way of legislative change occurred in the nearly three months of his administration. Six Bills were passed. The *Commonwealth Conciliation and Arbitration Bill* saw various amendments carried and defeated, but the Bill had not found passage through the parliament to become an Act.[12] The government was defeated 36-34 on a procedural vote to ensure this draft legislation allowed preference for unionists in awards. This defeat occurred on 13 August 1904. Watson wrote a four-page letter to the Governor-General requesting a dissolution of the House of Representatives. He pleaded:

> The leaders of the two other Parties have both declared that responsible government is impossible with three parties nearly equally divided. There seems little hope that a stable administration can be formed from amongst those opposed to the Government, and it would, therefore, be wise to afford the country an opportunity of giving one party an absolute majority at the polls.[13]

But Northcote declined to follow his Prime Minister's advice. In the archives is a Memo from Northcote, presumably the basis of advice both to Watson, Whitehall, and the King. Northcote's memo, *inter alia*, reads: "Having regard ... to the brief period which has elapsed since the last General Election", he felt "a General Election at the present moment does not appear to him to be essential in the public interest."[14] Holman concludes his assessment of the Watson government by remarking: "...the Arbitration Act, always a measure of ill-omen, was fated to be as disastrous to this Ministry as to others."[15] Holman then quoted a line from John Milton's poem *Lycidas*: "It was this fatal and perfidious bark. Built in eclipse and rigged with curses dark." The Bill, however, would be debated and dissected and amended and pass under the next government.

Instead of a dissolution of parliament, Reid was commissioned as Prime Minister, with the support of Deakin. Some of the radical Protectionists, Higgins and Isaacs included, informally supported, or loosely leaned towards Labor. Deakin, with mixed emotions, backed the Reid administration, partly because his friend and colleague Allan McLean sought office and became Deputy Prime Minister and Treasurer.[16] The Reid-McLean government, 1904-1905, was the beginning of realignment of the non-Labor parties. Largely at McLean's initiative, that government forced a vote and into law the *Conciliation and Arbitration Act* 1904. It was not everything Labor wanted, but as a grand compromise, it enshrined important reforms, including the widening of Commonwealth power to settle disputes (extended through subsequent High Court decisions), the registration of unions and employer associations and their 'standing' before the courts and administrative bodies to represent and be agents of employees or employers. This was important to the labour movement's growth and, through unions, to the extension of their coverage to most of the nation's employees.

Fitzhardinge's assessment of the Watson administration rings true:

> It was, to adopt Deakin's metaphor, a stone-walling innings, devoid of thrills for the spectator, if not for the batsmen, but it showed that the novice front bench could hold its wicket against the worst the veterans bowlers of both of the other teams could do, while the affairs of the country were quietly carried on without either red revolution or breath of a scandal.[17]

Freudenberg summed up the main achievement: "… the mere existence of a Labor Government, however brief, shone as a dawn of hope for the Labor Party everywhere."[18] The idea of Labor in government no longer seemed so monstrous a travesty.[19]

6

LEAVING THE PARLIAMENT FOR GOOD

An instructive exchange occurred between Watson and then aspiring Labor candidate James (Jimmy) Catts.[1] On 5 April 1906, Watson wrote to the latter urging him to look at seats other than Dalley, a Federal electorate that then covered inner suburbs of Sydney, including Balmain, Leichhardt and Glebe. Watson pointed out there were several new seats with new boundaries, including the then electorate of Cook whose boundaries covered the inner-Sydney suburbs of Redfern, Alexandria and Surry Hills. Watson explained: "Jack Grant[2] has a set of maps at the Trades Hall, & you could have a look at them."[3] Watson ended: "Trusting you will have a shot without bumping against a brick wall."[4] Catts replied the next day saying he had been approached for Dalley but would consider other options. He was about to go away for a fortnight, "but would like to have half an hour with you when I return."[5] Catts was convinced, stood for Cook, and was elected in 1906.

In the national election held on 12 December 1906, nominations were called for 75 seats and 68 were contested, with about 51.5% of the electorate voting. George Reid's Anti-Socialist Party (previously known as the Free Trade Party) won 27 seats and thereby displaced Alfred Deakin's Protectionists, who won 16 seats, as the largest non-Labor party. John Forrest's Western Australia Party won two. The Deakinites lost 10 seats, but four independent Protectionists supported them. With Labor's 26 seats, a Labor/Protectionist alliance enabled Deakin to remain Prime Minister from 1906 to 1908.

Five days after the 12 December 1906 elections, Watson wrote to Deakin: "I need hardly say that I am glad you were returned, as I thought it was a great mistake to run a man against you at all."[6] The candidate who ran for Ballaarat, Deakin's seat, was James Scullin, the future Labor Prime Minister. Before the election, the Free Trade candidate withdrew from the contest urging supporters to vote for Deakin. This was a precursor of the "fusion" of the anti-Labor parties, Free Trade, Protectionists, and others.

One test of any Australian Labor leader is in handling the party's platform and policy debates. For Watson, the national conferences of the party were personal and national: a mark of his stamina and personal stamp, a trial of direction and electability.

In 1905, for example, one of the most divisive issues was where the party stood on socialism, and whether more than monopolies should be brought under state control. The President of the Conference, Patrick Heagney,[7] boasted in a preface to the publication of its proceedings, that the conference "... evidenced the solidarity of Australian Labor and extinguished the last possibility of seriously dividing the Party."[8] Besides Watson, the other NSW delegates were John Grant, William Guthrie Spence, Hector Lamond, Donald Macdonell, and Edward Riley.

An important debate occurred on Labor's Objective, where Watson needed to use his wits and intelligence to thwart the simplistic appeal of 'socialism as nationalisation'. He had earlier convinced Cardinal Moran that Labor's 'milk and water' socialism could be tolerated by the Catholic Church. Pope Leo XIII's encyclical *Rerum Novarum*, 1891, supported unions, but explicitly condemned socialism. A hardline socialist policy of nationalisation would be opposed by the Church. Watson was acutely aware of this. Moran expressed a worldly pragmatism in saying in February 1905: "... if men in the advancement of their political interests choose the name Socialists, I say ... what's in a name if the false maxims of Communism are not adopted by those men."[9]

In this spirit, at the Conference, NSW and Tasmania put forward:

(a) The cultivation of an Australian sentiment based upon the maintenance of racial purity and the development in Australia of an enlightened and self-reliant community.

b) The securing of the full results of their industry to all producers by the collective ownership of monopolies and the extension of the industrial and economic functions of the State and the Municipality.[10]

A more sweeping proposition was moved by the Victorians: "The gradual nationalisation of the means of production, distribution, and exchange."[11] A slightly more elegant version of the Victorian proposal was advanced by the Queenslanders who proposed:

> That the objective of the Federal Labor Party should be declared, and in these terms: The securing of the results of their industry to all producers by the collective ownership of the means of production, distribution, and exchange, to be attained through the extension of the industrial and economic functions of the State and local governing bodies.[12]

Watson moved the NSW resolution. In his speech, Watson noted that: "It was a wise thing to direct the attention of the people to what they were really aiming at as a party."[13] In other words, what was under discussion was of vital importance. It was the rallying call of Labor to the nation. On the objective: "In fostering an Australian sentiment, he did not mean that it should be one over-bearing or arrogant, but that it should be cultivated in a true spirit of national pride."[14] Directly responding to the thrust of the Victorian and Queensland resolutions, Watson insisted: "It was sufficient that they were going for the collective ownership of monopolies, and understood their powers in that direction."[15]

Delegate James Fowler MHR from WA mocked the Queensland proposal: "It spoke of the 'collective ownership of the means of production, distribution, and exchange'. That would nationalise everything — the housewife's knitting needle and every laying hen."[16] Fowler went on to say: "He was a Social Democrat, and not a State Socialist, for with State Socialism they would have bureaucracy, red tape, and 'Government stroke' — three things which he believed would ruin everything."[17] Notwithstanding that Fowler eventually left the Labor Party in 1909, his words exemplified a strain of opinion from the earliest manifestation of Labor political initiative:. As much as Laborites wanted to curb the evil consequences of monopolies, there was a fear of the suffocating of initiative and of freedom by governmental bureaucracy.

Scots-born Tom Smeaton,[18] a MLA from South Australia, put matters pithily: "The highest definition of Socialism was 'Christianity applied'."[19] The vote was 23-11 in favour of the NSW/Tasmanian resolution, with Andrew Fisher voting with his Queensland colleagues in the minority.[20] After Labor policy was resolved, Moran's biographer noted that the Cardinal:

> ridiculed the efforts of George Reid… to confuse Labor's socialism with European communism. Watson wrote thanking [Moran] for his support of Labor's new socialist objective, one that recognised (in Watson's words) 'the frailty of human nature' and evidenced 'a willingness to pursue the Fabian policy. Of course, the extreme socialists are already denouncing the step as a retrograde one and are more than ever opposed to the Labor party as half-hearted. Still, in view of reforms already achieved, each lightening the load a little, we can afford to ignore the blind enthusiasts'.[21]

The socialist debate was not the end of controversy at the Labor conference of 1905.

A debate erupted on whether Labor should align with Deakin's protectionist liberals. Consideration of this issue boiled to the surface concerns about how Watson's ministry was decided in 1904. It brought Watson into conflict with his party on the role and powers of the parliamentary Labor Leader. Watson's strategy of alliance with the progressive Liberal protectionists was under attack. Watson thought there was an important governance issue at stake:

> … the view he took was that the organisations outside laid down the policy upon which the Party was to work and decided what the platform should be. They arranged the pledge for each candidate to take before he submitted himself for election. But once the man was in Parliament, they had to carry out their work. The alliance at any rate

prevented a fusion of the two other parties, who could thus have presented a solid phalanx to Labor. The question of an alliance would only be determined by the immediate circumstances of the case. The alliance which they had made had more than justified itself.[22]

But the Conference decided: "That the Federal Labor Party should not enter into any alliance that would extend beyond the then existing Parliament, nor grant nor promise immunity from opposition at election time."[23]

Another debate with potential to 'go the wrong way' in Watson's view centred on unimproved land values tax. The flamboyant, opinionated King O'Malley explained it was only the large property owners they had in mind: "They did not want to touch the little bantams — it was the big, gilded roosters of the brahmapootra [Brahmaputra] order they wished to get at."[24] Senator George Pearce, WA, had moved: "That an unimproved land values tax without exemption be a plank in the Federal Fighting Platform". But Hector Lamond successfully moved an amendment that, instead, they agree to "a progressive land values tax." The Conference report suggests that the Labor Leader became exasperated:

> Mr Watson said that the members of the Conference in the rush of enthusiasm were prepared to pile handicaps on the party. At the present time they had a big fight to carry on in the cry of Socialism v. anti-Socialism, and that would require all their energies. They had their Socialistic objective to aim for, and whilst he was glad to be one to bear the burden of the fight, he trusted that the burden would not be too heavily increased at this juncture …[25]

No national Labor Leader could take for granted a Labor Conference. Watson had to harness all his energies, policing the wording of nearly every clause, cajoling the delegates to consider not only what was right to do, but how to sell an idea to the electorate, and be mindful of practical questions like how far ahead of public opinion could an idea be taken and pursued.

In the aftermath of that conference, Watson wrote a letter of resignation to his colleagues. He disagreed with caucus electing the ministry rather than the Leader appointing the ministers. And Watson believed the leader should have discretion in forging parliamentary alliances and agreeing to forgo contests in certain electorates, where for example, a sympathetic liberal had a better chance of winning. Watson was hurt by the resolution on alliances. His letter to colleagues on 27 July 1905 said: "I am compelled to regard one of the resolutions as a censure upon the Labor Party in the Federal Parliament and another as a censure upon myself."[26] He went on:

> Once the Party enters Parliament it alone should, by its corporate voice, decide the course to be taken in any particular emergency. Having chosen its captains, the party outside should be prepared to trust to their guidance while the battle continues. If they do wrong, that is a reason for selecting fresh men when an election comes round; but I contend that the men in Parliament are, or should be, the best equipped to deal with Parliamentary emergencies.[27]

He complained: "…what other party would ally itself with us if, at the ensuing election, it had not only to fight the common enemy but also run the risk of being shot from behind."[28] Watson warned that the policy would "seriously handicap those entrusted with the work of translating principles into Parliamentary enactments."[29]

He ended his missive: "In conclusion, I desire only to add my belief in our Party is undiminished, and that, conceiving it to be the only Party likely to materially benefit the great majority of the people, I shall always be found in its ranks."[30] Watson was persuaded to withdraw his resignation.

At the 1906 Federal election, Watson again led Labor, increasing its votes and seats in the parliament. Watson was co-author of a Liberal-Labor agreement which lay the foundation of significant reforms. Watson felt it better to prop up Deakin as Prime Minister despite Labor being the larger party. In combination, the two could enact reforms that Labor on its own was incapable of achieving. In

October 1907, Watson resigned as Labor leader in favour of his Deputy, Andrew Fisher. Thereafter, the new Labor Leader enjoyed a free hand to criticise and cajole the Deakin administration, within the bounds of an informal alliance with the Protectionists. But Deakin was wary of Fisher in a way he had not been about Watson. It was not a paradisaical relationship. The tension in their relationship calls to mind the Woody Allen quip: in Heaven The lion and the calf shall lie down together but the calf won't get much sleep.[31]

Post-Labor leadership, but while still an MP, one decision on which Watson decisively took the lead was the location of the national capital. Though initially favouring Tumut (in early 1904), he later shifted his view to Canberra.[32] In 1908, the vote was between Canberra or Dalgetty. Watson led the argument for the winning side.[33] A fishing trip, years before, and his informal surveying of the capital region, convinced him.[34]

On 6 November 1908, Fisher advised Deakin that Labor would no longer support the government. Sawer notes:

> There was no immediate specific cause for this decision. It resulted from an accumulation of minor dissatisfactions, from a growing feeling that Labor could give effect to its own policy better through a government from its own ranks, and from an appreciation of the inappropriateness of Deakin's sixteen being supported by Labor's twenty-seven, rather than vice versa.[35]

Deakin advised the Governor General to call on Fisher. Watson declined to serve in the Fisher ministry. He wanted to give the new Prime Minister a free hand. Already, Labor's first Prime Minister was contemplating life outside of politics.

Watson's restless energy propelled him far from the regular homelife that Mrs Watson had dreamed of. Not much is known about Mrs Ada Watson, notwithstanding that she had 15 years of experience as a 'political wife' including, of course, when her husband was Prime Minister. From 1901, J.C. Watson spent long periods away in Melbourne, where the Parliament sat, as well as campaigning and travelling across the country. It took Watson 24-hours by train to travel between Melbourne and their Sydney home. Mrs Watson's thinking was probably a factor in her husband's retirement from Labor leadership in 1907 and ultimately from the parliament in 1910. A 1907 newspaper report mentions that a Labor Party women's delegation met with Mrs Watson at her home at 12 Bent Street, Paddington, to urge her husband to continue as Leader: "But when the case was stated to her, she said simply, 'I don't care about power or pay, position or Parliament; I only want what you women all want, my husband at home with me.'" The report concluded: "The reply was irresistible, and the women who came to plead remained to sympathise."[36] It is not known whether, as a seamstress, she was an active unionist in her 20s and 30s like many Sydney women in the clothing trades. Not even a photograph of Ada Watson can be found.[37]

Watson's visit to South Africa in 1909 turned into a nine-months sojourn managing a gold mine for the mining entrepreneur, William Tewksbury,[38] and his interests in the northeast of the country, near the border with modern-day Zimbabwe. Thankfully, for Labor's interests, Watson was 'paired' with a conservative MP (usually Reid), during absences from the parliament.

After the non-Labor parties merged in May 1909, the following month, Deakin was recalled as Prime Minister, with Joseph Cook as his Deputy. Four of Deakin's former MHR colleagues refused to support the new administration, aligning informally with Labor without joining or seeking to join them. The two-party system, ending the 'three elevens' had come into being. The interregnum between the Prime Ministerships of Deakin, 1906-1908, then Fisher 1908-1909, was followed by fusion of the non-Labor parties on 26 May 1909. Deakin was defeated by Fisher in the elections held in 1910. Labor had come of age, positioned to win, and winning outright that year.

Watson's-long-continued absence in South Africa furnished La-

Mr Watson in South Africa, *The Australasian* [Melbourne Victoria], 24 July 1909, p. 222.

bor's opponents with a brick to throw for all it was worth. Watson took most of his last 12 months' parliamentary salary without attending to the needs of his local electorate. He was mostly overseas, in South Africa. Some Fusionists were reportedly confident that Watson's action would cause the loss of enough votes to enable them to win his seat.[39]

Before the 13 April 1910 Federal elections, Watson gave various speeches, some clearly in response to speculation about his 'real reasons' for quitting politics, explaining his reasons for doing so, and in defence of his old party. He had not made a fortune in South Africa, he said. In one speech in February 1910, it was reported:

> Mr. Watson stated that as to the things which had been said about him, he could not confirm the statement about his increase in wealth. That had not happened. …He was afraid that he had not yet struck that golden shower which was supposed to put one beyond monetary anxiety, although they all, of course, lived in hopes.[40]

Another instance, in early March 1910 at the Waterloo Town Hall speaking in support of his successor as the endorsed ALP candidate for South Sydney,[41] Watson said "it was because his health had broken down" that he was leaving although, "He was never in fuller sympathy with the aims and objects and methods of the Labor party than he was to-day. Its methods were admittedly not perfect, but there was no party with a programme so attractive or so earnest," referencing its reform agenda on compulsory military training, a progressive land tax, and other policy.[42] On machine politics, Watson said Labor's methods were now being emulated, as the recent election of the Speaker in the Federal parliament and the selection of candidates of the Commonwealth Liberal Party illustrated. On the discipline of the Labor MPs, he remarked on another occasion: "Personally he could see no objection whatever to the caucus. It was a practice found necessary when the Labor party first came into existence, because they saw that to make their small voice heard at all, it was essential they should vote as one man on every question."[43]

Watson continued to play an active role in the Labor party, with the NSW ALP Executive, presiding sometimes in the absence of its officers.[44]

7

The Short Triumph of Labourism

The idea of Labor candidates formally supported by the unions had been floated for years at the Sydney Trades and Labour Council.[1] At a meeting on 11 March 1890 of the Council's Parliamentary Committee, attended by Watson, the Council's President, Peter Joseph Brennan spoke at length about organising a new party. That meeting resolved that any candidate expecting Council support needed to be a financial member of the relevant union and proposed that "any person accepting the labour platform and pledging himself to vote in favour of such measures [should] receive the support of the Trades and Labour Council."[2]

Agreement was thereafter reached on the NSW Labor Platform:

1. Abolition of plural voting.
2. Free and compulsory education.
3. Legalisation of the eight-hour system.
4. A Workshops' and Factories' Act and the appointment of representative working-men as inspectors.
5. Greater protection to persons engaged in the mining industry.
6. Extension of the franchise to seamen and shearers.
7. Extension to seamen of the benefits of the Employers' Liability Act.
8. Supervision of land boilers and machinery.
9. An elective Upper House.
10. Any measure that will secure for the wage-earner a fair and equitable return for his or her labour.
11. Amendment of the *Masters and Servants Act*.
12. Amendment of the *Masters and Apprentices Act*.

13. Amendment of the *Trade Union Act*.
14. Invalidation of agreements between Master and Man made outside the colony.[3]

This was a labourist manifesto of a political party seeking to influence politics, through practical, realistic, and compelling objectives. After the 'fusion' of the non-Labor parties in 1909, Labor gained traction and broadened its base to attract erstwhile radical and moderate liberals.[4] The party's golden age was beginning. Confident expressions of 'labourism', as to what the movement stood for, in contrast to conservatism, socialism, communism and liberalism, peppered the rhetoric of Labor politicians and Labor newspapers.

Except for Victoria, where the lingering influence of Deakinite liberalism buoyed the anti-Labor vote, at state level Labor majority governments were formed in South Australia (13 April 1910), NSW (14 October 1910), Western Australia (3 October 1911), Queensland (22 May 1915) and Tasmania (3 June 1925). Victoria finally followed suit on 6 December 1952. Nationally, at the fourth federal general election on 13 April 1910 Labor won 43 of the 75 House of Representatives seats and obtained a clear majority in the Senate (23 of 36 seats). Labor's successes eluded equivalent social democratic and labour parties in other countries for many years. This was the brief triumph of Australian labourism, an explicitly stated ideology, which held until the conscription split of 1916.

Watson was deeply involved in the development of a coherent, new political force, and its messaging. In April 1891, Plumbers' Union and Labor Council official John West[5] and Watson set up the Labor Electoral League in West Sydney.[6] Ellis notes: "When Henry Parkes dissolved Parliament in the following June (1891) J.C. Watson was the name of the League's honorary secretary in West Sydney, strenuously supporting the candidature of inter alia the *Bulletin*'s red-headed poet, [Edwin James] Brady,"[7] who, however failed to win pre-selection. Instead, the electorate returned four Labor men: J. "Jack" D. Fitzgerald,[8] George Black, Andrew Joseph Kelly,[9] and Thomas Martin Davis,[10] in that order. They were four of the 35 Labor NSW MLAs elected on the party's first electoral showing in 1891.

Labor, in its first quarter of a century, its formative era, had an appreciation for the tension between liberty and tradition, including existing institutions and values. The party's actions and stances as expressed by their MPs showed they assessed that amelioration, rather than expropriation or extirpation, ought to be the default reform approach; the party was inclined to support more significant change only where there was appreciation for the good that ought to be retained or amended; and it sought to extend the sphere of liberty of working people and the community more generally, and independence of action in their reform agenda.[11] Such principles were characteristic of moderate, positive public policy reform with commensurate action.

The birth of an Australian labour movement confident about its potential to effect change benefitted from a relatively liberal environment, despite determined and sometimes ferocious opposition. Many tributaries led to the formation of the Australian labour movement. Although its impulses were sometimes utopian, with dreamy romanticism mixed with hard-nosed industrial unionism, all was forged into a political movement.[12] In Arthur Griffith's[13] words: "The Labor Party of New South Wales stands for that commonsense Socialism which goes step by step, taking one plank of reform and nailing it down securely, and then going on and taking another and doing the same with it."[14]

William Lane, founder of the Brisbane *Worker* newspaper, was embittered and in despair after the iron-heel of the state crushed the workers during the great strikes of the early 1890s. As he, passengers, and crew sailed out of Sydney Harbour on 16 July 1893 on the *Royal Tar*, from the wharves came cheers and waves. One of those with Lane, James Molesworth, on his way to Cosmos in Paraguay, a subscriber to the New Australia Co-operative Settlement Association, the working man's paradise, as they envisaged, later starkly conveyed the contrast between the naïve, idealist settlers sailing to Latin America, and the pragmatists who stayed behind: "There were two schools of Labor thought. One – headed by W.A. Holman, J.C. Watson, G.S. Beeby, and W.M. Hughes – urged that Australia was the Workingman's Paradise, but that the worker had lost it. Political action was necessary to regain it."[15] Many of the voyaging utopians, like Molesworth, would one day regret the adventure.[16]

On a Sunday in early March 1902, Watson spoke at the Richmond Town Hall, Melbourne, on the 'Ethics of Labor Legislation'. What was described by the Melbourne *Age* correspondent as "a large audience" came to hear the Labor leader speak on an issue that interested activists and supporters, quiet believers and the curious: Could the work of the labour movement be considered ethical, and if so, in what sense? They came not only for inspiration, but also to answer the call of the local Workingmen's Club to raise a collection in aid of Frank Barber "afflicted with blindless" and "in indigent circumstances".[17] Watson surely remembered his blind stepfather's situation. The Labor MLA for Fitzroy, John Bilson,[18] said "if society were formed on a proper, humanitarian basis, there would be no necessity to make such appeals to individual charity. The care of its citizens was the first duty of the State, that none should become the victims of want and misery."[19]

Accounts of his speech[20] cite Watson's quote from Jeremy Bentham who said that ethics is "the art of directing men's actions to the production of the greatest quantity of happiness."[21] Watson argued that the Labor Party's "objects and measures" were inspired by "the ethical idea to do right to their brothers as well as themselves." Watson contended every law "more or less" infringed on the liberty of the individual. 'How far should they go?' was the question. In his view, "just as far as the circumstances practically seemed to warrant, and just as far as was likely to be successful." Although the Labor Party could be said to represent those "who laboured as distinguished from those who loafed," he proposed that the party's achievements were "conducive to the well-being of the community, as a whole." What was achieved "stood out as a beacon to the world today."[22] Although, always, there is a struggle to reach a better future. Watson insisted that what the movement had achieved needed to be understood:

> Though never strong enough to take into its own hands the reins of Government, it had at least acted as the pacemaker for every other party. The factories and old age pensions legislation – which was by no means as complete as it ought to be owed existence to the Labor party. This legislation was an object lesson to the whole world.

With an eye to his audience and the pitiable circumstances of Mr Barber there, Watson said:

> Old age pensions should be granted as a right, not as a matter of charity. By paying a little extra taxation the taxpayer could ensure himself in his old age a pension in a much more economical manner than by paying into the best of life insurance companies, in which the cost of collecting premiums was from 10 to 12 per cent.

Interestingly, Watson said he and colleagues were sometimes asked where was to be the end of the Labor party's efforts? Watson replied: "Frankly, … there was no end; the movement would go on… So long as wealth and want marched side by side would there be the necessity for agitation." Those words call to mind the German Social Democrat revisionist Eduard Bernstein's words in January 1898: "I frankly admit that I have extraordinarily little feeling for, or interest in, what is usually called 'the final goal of socialism'. This goal, whatever it may be, is nothing to me, the movement is everything."[23] There is no evidence that Watson read anything by Bernstein or followed the evolution of German Social Democrat thinking away from doctrinaire Marxist ideas, but it is interesting that Watson reached a similar conclusion. *The Tocsin* reported Watson saying: "Every hill scaled in the march of human progress only disclosed fresh views and vistas. Every labour movement, under its own name or another, would be animated by the spirit of humanity, and agitation would cease only with the end of time itself."[24] Watson greeted his audience's hopes with inspiration, words rolling from the stage to irrigate their lives. The occasion ended with the Richmond City brass band's selections, several vocal solos, and the collection for Mr. Barber, £9.00.

One of Watson's most significant speeches, on Socialism, was delivered in the Unitarian Church Liverpool Street, Sydney, in early 1905. There are various reports of Watson's speech, the longest of which began with a poem:[25]

> Oh, he preached it from the housetops,
>   and he whispered it by stealth;
> He wrote whole miles of stuff against
>   the awful curse of wealth;
> He shouted for the poor man,
>   and he called the rich man down.
> He roasted every king and queen
>   Who dared to wear a crown.
> He hollered for rebellion,
>   and he said he'd head a band
> To exterminate the millionaires,
>   to sweep them from the land.
> He yelled against monopolies,
>   took shots at every trust,
> And swore he'd be an anarchist,
>   to grind them in the dust.
> He stormed, he fumed and ranted,
>   till he made the rich men wince,
> But an uncle left him money,
>   and he hasn't shouted since.

Those words might have set the mood for the reader, but I doubt that Watson's oration would have commenced that way.

Nairn's *Civilising Capitalism* tells the story of the part played by the trade unions in NSW in forming the parliamentary Labor Party in 1891 at a time when triumphant capitalism was lurching out of control. Nairn wrote his opus to account for Labor's history and to rebut the charge that the Labor Party had failed as a revolutionary party and was fatally compromised as a party of reform. Labor was never other than reformist, seeing its mission as civilising, not killing the socio-economic system it co-habited with.

In a beautifully written snapshot, Nairn presents a picture of NSW Labor at the end of the nineteenth century:

> By 1898, a peculiar aura, produced by an amalgam of comradeship, controlled bickering, and missionary fervour, enfolded the Labor Party and conditioned a special type of colonist. For the most part he was a member of a league, but not necessarily; and, generally, he was a member of a trade union, but not invariably. But always he voted Labor. A 'Labor man' owed a lot to the trade union tradition of purposeful solidarity, originally shaped in the city by constant pressure to improve working conditions, but effortlessly absorbed by the bush unions from the middle 1880s and given a new dimension by the shrewd inarticulateness and warm generosity that was part of the lonely country life. The Labor Party linked the city with the country, in a way no other organisation could hope to because it was the crown of a movement that held out the prospect of a better life for all people who found life hard. The Labor Party offered a chance to all colonists, irrespective of their background and education, to become significant people as they shared in a common socially curative task. A league president or secretary was a person of local importance, a conference delegate more so, the executive officers of the PLL were colonial figures; Labor members of the Legislative Assembly were men of power and authority. The lowliest league member, or even just a Labor voter, could share

in the system that made these men; and he knew that he would not be overwhelmed by them, indeed if necessary he might be able to organise support that could destroy them; and he knew that Jim McGowen or Chris Watson were leaders who belonged to him and were answerable to him, not leaders who had the ascendancy and the will to scorn him, even should one of them become the premier of New South Wales or the prime minister of Australia, as were possibilities for all 'Labor men' looking forward from 1898. The turn of the 'Labor woman' would come early in the twentieth century.[26]

When Watson retired from politics in 1910, Labor won office outright in the Federal and NSW Parliaments. The slow, patient method of presenting Labor's agenda through bargains with non-Labor parties, improvements through concessions, gave way to the party governing on its own.

This required explanation to supporters. And to some foreigners interested to explore Antipodean socialist experiments. Many of those, perplexed by the non-ideological pretensions of Australian Laborites interpreted this as 'socialism without doctrines' (*Le socialisme sans doctrines*), in Frenchman Albert Métin's felicitous phrase.[27]

In the German socialist press, opinions varied between admiration for what Australian Laborites had wrangled out of the capitalist system, to despair at the 'backwardness' and lack of class consciousness of Australian socialists and social reformers.[28] Métin wrote before Labor achieved outright success in any Australian (or New Zealand) parliament, and had only won concessions from minority administrations propped up by Labor votes on the principle of "Support in Return for Concessions."[29] One of the first Labor MPs elected to the NSW Parliament, George Black,[30] journalist and politician, one of the pioneers of the NSW Labor Party and its most prolific and insistent early chronicler, articulated this position and in 1891 was identified as "the principal spokesman on behalf of the party" on the tactic.[31]

Black's chief works on NSW ALP history were various editions of his *History of the NSW Labor Party. From Its Conception till Now*,[32] and a pamphlet, *Labor in Politics: the New South Wales Labor Party: What it Did and What it Prevented*, in various editions.[33] Black's contribution to Australian labour history is neglected. His similar sounding titles, numerous editions thereof, his chequered political history, and expulsion from the party, and his various reinterpretations, which shifted from eulogising to disillusionment, meant that the best of his explication of what Labor stood for and why it did so has hitherto mostly escaped critical attention.

One chapter of his *History* headed 'The Charges Against Laborism Refuted' is a robust defence of NSW Labor politics.[34] Black saw the need to articulate a position in contradistinction to "… the dust kicked up by the heels of sectarian, fiscal and one idea-ed cranks, or by the splatterdashes of a capitalism intent always on disguising the real issues either in politics or in industrialism."[35] Black also had in mind socialist and leftwing criticisms.

His colleague in the West Sydney election victory of 1891, Jack Fitzgerald, lamented in 1915 that Black's *History* was "too little read even in our own Party."[36] Labor was more than what its politicians did. Labor expressed itself in moderately radical proposals and evolved its own codes of custom, duty, and practice. The constituent parts were forged to a unity of purpose. This, however, could not obscure that the parts were more than the whole. There would always be tension between the parliamentarians, the union leaders, the activists, the political rank and file, and the public. Nairn explains the complexities of Labor's internal politics:

> The executive was the focal point of a mass political party that expressed a deeply rooted striving for comprehensive reform; while, to a degree, the executive was insensitive to the intricate nature of the problems of Labor parliamentarians, it could not allow itself to be engulfed by them; that way led to stagnation, and a primary objective of the Labor strife of 1891-4 was to avoid that. Nor could the execu-

tive afford to give the impression to league members that it would follow the pace set by Assembly members; the rank and file regarded it as their spokesman and the custodian of right Labor principles and practice. The executive had to assert some authority over the parliamentarians, both to placate ordinary members of the PLL and to ensure that Labor members of the Legislative Assembly should never rest on their oars with the feeling that the race was over. In fact, the whole Party had started on a contest that would never be won. And part of the game was the difficulty of each section of a complex Party in recognising and appreciating the problems of other sections: this poser applied particularly to relations between those inside parliament and those outside, but it was also apparent, in the personal tension inherent in the bonds that linked in perpetual dynamism the institutional sections of the Party, executive, assemblies, branches and conference, as well as the trade unions.[37]

In that crisp summary, the dynamic and dynamism of Labor leadership can be detected. As party leader, Watson was more than the public face of the movement. He had to keep everyone as aligned as possible. This required a mastery of personality, principles, purpose, and presentation. Each part of the movement had leaders and influencers who needed to know they were recognised and heard. Watson's political career lived up to the ethics of responsibility that Weber described as one of two main courses a politician's life might take. Replying to points made on the socialist objective debate at the 1905 national conference of the ALP, Watson declared:

> … they as a Party had much more to do for the people than the mere looking out for a seventh heaven for them. They as managers of the labour movement had to direct their forces in such a way as to obtain every possible, reasonable, and immediate result. The whole history of the labour movement in Australia had been not the attitude of "crying for the moon," but to accept what was practical and immediate. He considered that the success of the Labor Party had been brought about not through following out theoretic ideas,

but because they recognised that this or that measure advocated by them was something immediately tangible."[38]

What Black called curing 'The Things That Are', what Watson saw as tangible, reasonable, and possible results to aim for, were all characteristic of NSW Labor.

Watson did not possess the analytical, critical mind of German social democrat theorist and MP Eduard Bernstein. In reaching his conclusions about piecemeal reform, however, Watson had thought about socialist principles and theory (he read widely, had participated in various socialist societies, and heard and participated in debates within the Australian labour movement about socialism).[39] His parliamentary experience convinced him that reforms could be won through democratic means. In this assessment, Watson's conclusions are similar to Bernstein's. The latter stated:

> I discarded as irrelevant the notion that the final goal and practical reform work are mutually exclusive – without encountering any protest – and I agreed that for England a further peaceful development … is at least not improbable. I expressed the view that if free development were to continue, the English working class would certainly increase its demands, but would not demand anything which could not always be shown to be unquestionably necessary or attainable. That is at bottom nothing other than what I say today. And if anyone wishes to bring against me the progress Social Democracy has achieved in England since then, I reply that this expansion has been accompanied, and, made possible, by English Social Democracy's development from a utopian-revolutionary sect, as Engels himself repeatedly represented it to be, into a party of practical reform.[40]

Similarly, Watson's focus on Australian Labor as a party of practical and pragmatic reform was his life's driving ambition.

8

THE UNSETTLED BARGAIN ON NATIONAL DEFENCE

Watson's views on defence policy matured as he grew to understand the challenges of defending an island continent. In his early days in the Australian parliament, he queried whether too much was being spent on defence. But within a year, he changed his tune and with William Morris Hughes became the master of Australian Labor's defence policy. Meaney says Watson aligned "himself with the preparedness lobby."[1]

Watson's early attitude was exemplified in a sketch in the Melbourne press in October 1902, mostly expressing reservation about his 'influence':

> Sir William Lyne said he had done all that a man could do in cutting down the defence estimates, but when Mr. Watson said "You must knock another £62,000 off this, he meekly replied, "Could you not see your way to halve it, just for this year. It is awkward, you know, to retrench money that you have already spent. You see the difficulty, don't you?" So Mr. Watson consciously consented to allow the further cutting down of the "military toffs" to stand over till the new year. But he was peremptory in his orders, "Let there be no mistake about it. I mean what I say, there must be a real retrenchment." And the Minister delighted at getting a reprieve said, "Yes, Mr. Watson! Certainly Mr Watson!"[2]

A visit to the Northern Territory and other parts in 1907 he concluded the defence of Australia needed more people, more British migrants, especially to "our most vulnerable point while, distant a few days steam, cluster the myriads of Asia, threatening ever to swarm across ..."[3] Reflecting in 1914 on the evolution of Labor's approach to Australia's defence, Watson wrote:

The Labor Party's attitude towards Defence has undergone an immense change since its first entrance into politics. In 1890 the NSW platform (there was little variation in the other colonies) proposed the "establishment of our military system upon a purely voluntary basis", as against the mixed militia and permanent system then prevailing."[4]

He explained: 'The wider outlook necessitated by the responsibility of caring for the affairs of a continent had its most important influence in regard to defence."[5]

In August 1906, Watson set out his thinking for the journal of the Australian National Defence League (ANDL):

… we must sooner or later expect to be face-to-face with the necessity of defending ourselves against aggression. The pressure of population in the older parts of the world, and the awakening of what is colloquially known as "the East," constitute at least a potential menace to any people situated as we are. Our wide areas of unpeopled territory, rich with unrealised possibilities, must inevitably prove an attraction to nations confined within boundaries too small for the natural expansion of their populations.[6]

Noting that although most might agree in the abstract with such analysis, Watson asked: "What, then, should be done?" He answered:

Leaving aside detail, we should immediately initiate a system of coast defence, aiming at the provision of safe havens along the coast for our merchant shipping and bases for the Imperial fleet; factories should be established for the manufacture of small arms and ammunition; and, above all, we should take steps to ensure training in the use of arms and the simpler military evolutions, [of] our adult male population. Military training and the provision of arms for all citizens is essential to the maintenance of our civic liberties, and none should hesitate because of the comparatively small sacrifice involved.[7]

The ANDL was founded "on strictly non-party lines" and "its political action" was "directed to influence members of every party to support" the "aims and objects" of the League.⁸ Details of policy were outlined in issues of *The Call*. The 2 November 1906 issue reported the League's 'Objects' as:

> To take such measures as may be necessary and proper to secure:
>
> (a) Universal compulsory training (military or naval) of the boyhood and manhood of Australia for purposes of National Defence, the military training to be on the lines of the Swiss system, and the naval training on the lines of the British Royal Naval Reserve, modified to suit local circumstances.
>
> (b) An adequate and effective system of National Defence.⁹

Confidently expressed as were the opinions of the writers for the League, it was not easy to win support for them. At the annual meeting of the League in September 1907, however, Watson noted a favourable shift in mood in the Australian parliament:

> ... he was glad to find that the leaders of the other two great parties in the Federal House, Mr Deakin and Mr Reid, had both lately given utterance to very sympathetic remarks in reference to the main principles upon which the League was fighting; and he was encouraged to hope from their attitude that when the motion of Mr W.M. Hughes in favour of compulsory military training came to the vote, there would be a reasonable prospect of a majority in its favour.¹⁰

Watson saw defence policy as intricately associated with social reform. Even with respect to the recent passage of legislation for the age pension. In November 1908, after he had relinquished party leadership, but was still an MP in the Federal Parliament, he argued "security is essential to progress"¹¹ and suggested: "The passage by the Federal Parliament of a law providing for the payment of old-age and invalid pensions throughout Australia seems a fitting occasion to inquire whether the new law should not involve as a necessary corollary the adoption of universal military service."¹² He saw action by the young in training for the defence of the realm as related to privileges in old age:

> The young man who has prepared himself to take part effectively in defence, and thus helped to guarantee the stability of the Commonwealth, has made a distinct and valuable contribution to the resources of the community … It is just as important to retain as to obtain reforms; therefore "resistance to the invader" is the natural complement of "assistance to the aged" …[13]

This debate within the Labor Party was still controversial, though a majority favoured compulsory training along Swiss lines, but *not compulsory conscription*. The 1908 Conference of the ALP featured debates on the merit of a training policy. Proudly, the League noted:

> One of our Vice-Presidents, Mr J.C. Watson, MHR, took the initiative by moving a resolution in favour of the principle of compulsory military training, which was ultimately passed by a majority of 24 to 7 in the following form:- "That the following be substituted for the present plank: 'Citizens' Defence Force, with compulsory military training, and Australian owned and controlled navy.'"
>
> A further plank, on the motion of Mr Catts, was put and carried by 29 votes to 3, in this form – "that military and naval expenditure be allotted from proceeds of direct taxation."[14]

Those resolutions became the highpoint of pro-compulsory training policy within the ALP. They were guidance for what the Andrew Fisher-led Labor Party would strive to effect during his leadership as Australian Labor Leader, 1907-1915.

In 1908 at the national ALP conference, however, Tasmanian MHR King O'Malley contested the consensus and "wondered if the Labor Party had gone mad on militarism. Labor had been fighting for justice and freedom, and now they proposed to adopt the most diabolical methods of Europe."[15] Even W.A. Holman, who eight years later would quit the ALP on the conscription issue, was reported to say that "though he supported Mr Watson's resolution, he did so without the slightest enthusiasm …"[16] Senator Ted Findley (Victoria) "reminded the Conference that the Australian Labor

The front cover of the Australian National Defence League's *The Call*, No. 3, February 1907. The ideals of the ANDL Watson fully supported.

Party, anterior to Federation, was a peace party …"[17] Lamond, on the other hand, said he "was in favour of preparing for war, because he was a firm believer in peace."[18] As for O'Malley's claim, Watson in reply to the debate said: "… he would again point out that this proposal would, in the very nature of things, be anti-militarism …", explaining further that trustfulness and lack of preparation would make aggression one day more likely.[19] In a note to the summary of the debate in *The Call*, Watson said the "Citizens' defence force" required "that every year [each eligible] man shall undergo some training."[20]

At the end of 1914, Prime Minister Fisher asked Watson to travel to the UK, Canada, and New Zealand, and he left for overseas a vigorous supporter of Australia's participation in the War. Fisher wanted Watson to be his representative and to personally appraise the war effort and to meet the Prime Ministers of Canada (Robert Borden), and New Zealand (William Massey), as well as UK Prime Minister (H.H. Asquith) and senior British ministers.

During this trip, Watson in April 1915 addressed an Imperial Parliamentary Association meeting at the House of Commons. He urged the British Government to summon an informal gathering of Dominion representatives as soon as practicable.[21] Watson had two ideas in mind. First, the need to ensure the British government was informed of and acted upon Australia's concerns about the post-War world. Second, as the fight in Europe involved the Empire, with troops from Australia, Canada, New Zealand, South Africa and elsewhere fighting, the governments of those countries should canvass common policies and aim to better co-ordinate the war effort. Watson expressed frustration at the condescending attitude of some of his UK Labour colleagues:

> Mr Snowden seems to regret that we in Australia did not approach the British Labour Party to ascertain its views on this matter, but though that might have been the counsel of perfection, it must be recognised that similar omissions have probably been made by Mr Snowden and his

colleagues in reference to matters of policy locally decided upon.[22]

This was a reference to another of Snowden's claims, namely: "… The Labour parties in these Colonies never approached the British Labour movement to ascertain what its views on the Imperial effect of this [compulsory military service] would be. So in regard to the naval policy of the Colonies. The Governments of the Colonies, Labour and otherwise, get all their ideas about naval policy from our official class."[23] Similarly, Snowden was wrong about Australian attitudes and Australian Labor's instigation of the Australian navy. Watson argued: "If we in Australia had followed the advice of the 'official class' there would now be no Australian navy. From the beginning of Federation in 1901 our Labor platform included a proposal for an Australian-owned navy."[24]

In his study of the conscription crisis in the ALP, Perks notes: "Labor defence policy prior to the conscription crisis of 1916 was almost entirely the creation of the federal caucus leaders in both general principles and detailed application as approved by the federal ALP structure."[25]

But all this was about to change and put to the test.

9

Conscription, Expulsion, and Aftermath

After all the good work of dragging itself into power outright, Labor risked its ruthlessly secured unity over the issue of conscription.

In late July 1914, a month after the Archduke Franz Ferdinand's assassination,[1] the Labor Leader Andrew Fisher said in a speech in Melbourne: "Should the worst happen, after everything has been done that honour will permit, we Australians will help and defend Britain to our last man and our last shilling. (Great cheering)."[2] The United Kingdom declared war on Germany on 4 August 1914[3] and therefore Australia too was at war.[4] Sir Joseph Cook was Prime Minister, fighting an election campaign, losing on 5 September 1914 to Fisher who for the third time became Prime Minister. Labor won almost 51% of the vote and 42 seats in the House, Cook's National Liberals won just over 42% of the vote and 32 seats. One Independent was also elected. Fisher's Labor administration immediately re-affirmed full support of the British war effort.

The Federal government established the Australian Imperial Force (AIF) at the outbreak of war and immediately began recruiting men to serve. They did so in the Middle East and on the Western Front. The AIF received huge numbers of applications to volunteer. Recruitment campaigns across the country were co-ordinated by the government and citizens' recruitment committees.

Fisher urged appreciation of what the Labor Party had prepared for the defence of Australia. His government had armed and equipped the army with up-to-date weapons, created the complex organisations necessary – including training colleges for officers and the instructional corps for the non-commissioned officers. The government commissioned, sponsored and/or encouraged small arms, ammunition, cordite, and accoutrement factories. Above all, the system of universal training through the Citizens' Defence Force was implemented.[5]

It had seemed that Labor's defence policy was broadly settled through Watson's studiously nuanced position at the 1908 Federal ALP Conference and the implementation of that policy by the Fisher governments from 1908-1909 and 1910-1913. But in politics, no victories survive unscathed by new tests and circumstances. They are renewed, reinterpreted, tolerated, discarded, or sabotaged.

In poor health, on 27 October 1915 Andrew Fisher resigned as Prime Minister, with Hughes unanimously elected by his colleagues as Labor Leader. In January 1916, the new Prime Minister, with the permission of caucus (the Labor party room), departed for London to discuss political and economic questions with the UK government, visiting New Zealand and Canada and their Prime Ministers along the way. Hughes sought to understand the progress of the war, the mobilisation effort across the British Empire, and he pressed Australia's political and economic claims. Returning on 31 July 1916, Hughes boasted that the British had agreed to purchase substantially more quantities of Australian wheat, wool, and metals. To enable this, on behalf of the government Hughes organised the purchase of ships for transport, the foundation of the government-owned Australian Shipping Line.[6]

The horrors of the Great War, the sacrifice and bravery of those Australians who had volunteered, the emerging Anzac legend, the news of deaths and casualties, were all at the forefront of the public's mind in 1916. Conscription for overseas service was a concept never agreed to previously by the party. What changed was that Labor leaders centred on Prime Minister Hughes feared German victory and sensed 'the Empire' was perilously close to losing, a propelling force leading to schism. A similar fear gripped the political leadership of the United Kingdom.

The Australian *Defence Act* only permitted men to be conscripted for military service within Australia, not for overseas service. Rumours that conscription for that purpose might be considered in Australia percolated throughout society. Conscription was introduced in Britain and New Zealand in the first half of 1916.[7] Would Australia act similarly? Australian voluntary recruitment declined during that year and did not fully replace the soldiers being killed and wounded on the Western Front.

Watson along with other leading lights across the spectrum believed in the necessity of conscription. The NSW Branch of the Universal Service League (USL) was formed in 1915 and Watson was one of many Vice Presidents,[8] including the Anglican and Catholic Archbishops of Sydney, Protestant pastors, the Chief Rabbi, conservative political figures, and Laborites including the NSW Premier William Holman, George Black, James Catts, Jack Fitzgerald, Arthur Griffith, and Dick Meagher.[9] Its Objects were:

> To advocate the adoption for the period of the present war of the principle of universal compulsory war service, whether at home or abroad; and to support the Government in providing at the earliest possible moment such Organization as is necessary to secure wise and just application of this principle.[10]

In blunter language: "Australia cannot be said to be doing her fair share unless she is doing her utmost."[11] Meaney speculates that Watson was a driving force behind the USL:

> It may well be that the British Round Table had induced the Sydney branch to follow their lead. It was remarkable that the Sydney movement was established so soon after the publication of the Manifesto in the *Times*, and especially so since the British Manifesto was only published in the Australian press in a very summary form which avoided all reference to conscription. Perhaps Watson, who had been in close touch with the Round Table during his visit to London in May [1915], was the conduit.[12]

In mid-September 1915 at the Labor Council of NSW, "A letter was read from the Universal Service League asking that a deputation, consisting of Professor Edgeworth David[13] and Mr. J.C. Watson, or Mr. H. Lamond, should be received by the delegates."[14] The executive of the NSW ALP anticipated a potential showdown, declaring in a resolution carried on 15 October 1915:

> That this executive of the PLL regrets that members have allowed the name of the League to be associated with their membership of the Universal Service League and expresses the opinion that it is inadvisable for members of the Labor movement to publicly associate themselves with controversial issues upon which the movement may be called upon to express an opinion.[15]

The wording of the resolution was menacing, and implied that until the NSW ALP executive ruled on the matter, prominent party members should keep their views to themselves, as if seeking support for a defined position was improper. The article in *The Australian Worker* which reported the resolution mentioned those of the PLL executive who were with the USL, namely Jack Fitzgerald (President), Dick Meagher (vice-president), NSW Premier Holman, George Lewis,[16] Claude Thompson,[17] and J.C. Watson.

Opposition brewed in anticipation of anything Hughes' and his ministers might be planning. At the May 1916 NSW Labor Conference, AWU union leader and former Senator Arthur Rae[18] successfully moved:

> That this conference solemnly pledges itself to oppose by all lawful means the conscription of human life for service abroad, and directs all affiliated unions and leagues to oppose all Labor members who vote for, or otherwise support conscription, so as to make this matter a clear-cut issue between the forces of democracy and despotism and where such action is taken the executive is authorised to refuse to endorse conscriptionist candidates.[19]

Rae was not anti-war. He opposed compulsion. Three of his sons served in the AIF. (Only one of those volunteers returned alive.) Rae's resolution ultimately led to a wave of ALP expulsions over conscription.

[PASTE UP.]   [READ OTHER SIDE.]

LABOR AND LOYALTY

In the Homes of Labor there is Patriotism and Love of Country

LABOR SENATE CANDIDATES:

PETER BOWLING
HAS
Five Sons on Active Service.

ARTHUR RAE
HAS
Two Sons on Active Service.
One Son in Camp Training.
One Son on Home Service.

SENATOR
DAVID WATSON
HAS
Two Sons on Active Service.

It is an insult to Australia's Soldiers to insinuate that Labor is disloyal. The above named Soldiers have not come from disloyal homes.

Vote for Labor No-Conscription for the Senate

Written by J. H. Catts, M.H.R., Director Labor Election Campaign. Authorised on behalf of the P.L.L. Executive by P. C. Evans, General Secretary. Worker Print, Sydney.   Macdonell House, Sydney.   [Over

Labor's NSW How to Vote Leaflet for the Senate in 1917, emphasising the patriotism of the Labor candidates.

Perks notes that calls for conscription stirred up opposition to recruitment campaigns as well as to Hughes' prognostications on compulsion:

> [The m]ajor effect upon the Labor movement generally was the marking of a shift from unenthusiastic support for the war to growing demands for withdrawal. Above all, the salient point which emerged was the attitude of the unions towards supporting the war effort ..."[20]

Within a political party constituted as was Labor, something, one of its parts, had to give.

The Labor Party split of 1916 centred on fundamental disagreements. Prime Minister Hughes became an enthusiastic supporter of conscription to boost Australia's contribution to the war effort. At a recruitment rally in August 1916 he thundered: "What is the good of prattling on about internationalism, while a wild beast roams abroad, to whom words are nothing and only foul deeds count."[21] On 30 August 1916, he announced plans for a referendum on the issue and introduced enabling legislation into parliament on 15 September 1916, which passed only with the support of the Opposition. Hughes sought a non-binding plebiscite to try and obtain a popular mandate; it was commonly referred to as a referendum. Six of his ministers resigned in protest at the move.

The Labor party, its membership, officers, and union leadership, still at home, decided that the party must direct its supporters as to what to do. On their calculation, the issues were too important to leave to everyone's conscience to decide. Indeed, the party insisted it could override individual conscience. For the losing side in the internal party debate, the consequences seemed outrageous and added to the embitterment. The leadership of the Political Labor League (the Labor Party organisation in NSW at the time) decided they had an obligation to take a stance. On 15 September 1916, the executive of the League expelled Hughes from the Labor Party. As Labor was then a federation of state parties, this did not immediately mean Hughes was no longer the Labor Prime Minister. But it was Limbo.

The referendum saw an intense campaign in which Labor figures vehemently advocated on each side of the argument.

A pro-conscription meeting at the Sydney Town Hall on 18 September 1916 was annoyed by the larger crowd outside, protesting. Inside: "Selections from 'Carmen', including the Song of the Toreador, filled out the time till two minutes to 8. At 8 o'clock a tempest of sound, shouting, cheering, whistling, and shrill cries of Coo-ee! Coo-ee! Announced the union of the man and the opportunity. The Prime Minister arrived"[22] and spoke.

> Immediately afterwards he was followed by another [speaker] almost as dramatic. [Hector] Lamond rose, placed [William Guthrie] Spence's grey felt hat on a chair and spoke: 'Only one man living in Australia has given such service to the industrial workers of this country as has the Prime Minister and he stands shoulder to shoulder with him in the course he is pursuing. That man is the venerable president of the Shearers' Union.[23]

It was a thunderclap moment. Lamond claimed that his father-in-law, Spence, was completely on-side with the Prime Minister. Tremendous cheering followed. Watson was on the stage with other conscription supporters.[24] He moved a vote of thanks, declaring:

> Some in this State with whom I have worked side by side ever since the beginning of the movement, and for whose opinion I have every respect, in whose bona fides I have every confidence, will persist in imagining that there is a chance of avoiding this service, and at the same time preserving our liberties. No such opportunity exists. The question is "which kind are we going to live?" I prefer being conscripted by my own fellow citizens, rather than by people like the Prussians, who would dragoon us to their way of thinking. The question to be resolved on October 28 comes back to this: Our men are there – they have suffered and died because of their enthusiasm in the cause of their country – shall we leave them unsupported? ("No, No." and cheers.)[25]

The language Watson used was pleading, respectful of opponents, insistent on the necessity of conscription. Outside the Town Hall, propelled to prominence,[26] the 25-year-old assistant secretary of the Boilermakers and Iron-shipbuilders' Society, Mr William McKell, who would one day be a pallbearer at Watson's funeral, declared:

> In no way can Monday's night meeting be taken as a true expression of the views of the workers in Sydney on the question of conscription. Thousands of workers attended only to find that the Town Hall doors were closed to them. Consequently, they held a meeting of their own, or one might say, meetings of their own and carried resolutions of their own against the Prime Minister's policy. The patriotic airs played in the hall to gain the sympathy of the crowd for Mr. Hughes may be quite proper, but they are not arguments. When Mr. Hughes' audience grows calm again and hears the wealth of arguments against conscription, they will realise that he is fighting with but a very bad case.[27]

After that meeting, the new NSW Labor Party President, Jack Doyle[28] declared he was minded that all pro-conscriptionist politicians should be expelled.[29] Hughes never stood long across the threshold. He ran towards the political cannon fire daring his opponents to cut down a Labor Prime Minister, with all the consequences. No-one blinked. The NSW Labor machine braced like an arrow drawn back – and released. Anti-conscription became a pledge issue for every NSW MP and supporter.

On 3 October 1916, with the Australia-wide referendum due at the end of the month, Watson dropped an incendiary bomb in a letter to *The Daily Telegraph* newspaper:

> It is marvellous how, under the stress of controversy, so many men lose their sense of logic. The attitude of some of our trade-union leaders on the conscription issue may be instanced. They admit that the war must be won, but the one great "argument" is that the Russians have plenty of men, and they should be relied upon to win for us. Leaving aside, for the moment, the fact that Russia is at present

utilising every man she can get into the firing line, let us examine the suggestion from the trade-union standpoint. As a unionist of over 30 years' standing, I have frequently seen the non-unionist refusing to assist in the struggle for better conditions, yet reaping the benefit after the victory was won. Our term for the man who did that, was terse though unpleasant – "Scab." Yet to-day some of our prominent trade-unionists, in and out of Parliament, are asking Australian unionists to "scab" on their fellow-workers in Russia and other Allied countries.

The idea is, "Let them pull the chestnuts out of the fire, and we'll do the eating!" I cannot believe the generous-hearted unionists of the Commonwealth will follow any such 'blackleg' principle. Our liberties are at stake in this fight equally with those of workers in Britain, France, or Belgium, and in common justice we must do our share towards victory. If we admit that Australian reinforcements must be sent to relieve or replace the brave men now in the trenches, how can they be secured except by compulsion?[30]

Comparing anti-conscriptionists to "scabs" was a low blow. Watson thought the charge completely justified.

Conscription held an outsize place in the Australian Labor psyche, beyond understandable immediate sympathy for the right of conscience and combatting 'militarism'. The issue became of overwhelming importance. Labor shook to its foundations. Many unionists, even some politicians, had volunteered to serve. They were therefore absent as the party shifted its positions. Freedom of conscience, principles of liberty, whether a volunteer army could maintain discipline and elan if conscripts were added to the mix, were issues to the fore.

The first conscription referendum was held on 28 October 1916. The question put to the Australian people was:

> Are you in favour of the Government having, in this grave emergency, the same compulsory powers over citizens in regard to requiring their military service, for the term of

this War, outside the Commonwealth, as it now has in regard to military service within the Commonwealth?

Before the vote, in a newspaper advertisement, Watson posted a personal plea:

> Australia's Honour
>
> To ensure Germany's defeat the Allies must utilise all their resources in men and munitions.
>
> Shall Australia be the first of the allied nations to hoist the white flag?
>
> Surely, we must help our boys at the front by sending adequate reinforcements and thus honour Australia's pledge.
>
> To preserve the Commonwealth as a white man's country, we must vote
>
> Y-E-S.
>
> J.C. Watson[31]

The referendum was defeated with 1,087,557 in favour and 1,160,033 against, a 3.2% margin. Western Australia, Tasmania, and, narrowly, Victoria, voted in favour. NSW voted over 57.0% against.

Hughes' stance and effort to quell dissent riled not just his hard-left enemies but also some allies and sympathisers who felt that calling for continued voluntary recruitment was in no sense a niggardly or disloyal response to the situation. As the political guillotine fell, Arthur Griffith asked that he and other Labor pioneers be spared obloquy. On 20 September 1916, Griffith said: "Notwithstanding what has happened … Mr Hughes, Mr. Holman, Mr. Watson, Mr. Lamond and myself, the five men who framed the Labor objective which has become the objective of both Commonwealth and State Labor parties, are still as strong Labor men as ever we were. The issue that separates us from our friends at present has nothing to do with either State politics or the Labor platform."[32] In early October, Watson at Ashfield, Sydney, at a public rally lamented that "some of his Labor friends said we had nothing at stake"[33] and proceeded to put the case why victory and compulsion mattered. This, once more, was Watson stating the case with an eye to persuading doubters and Laborites. After the October 1916 referendum, Griffith said that the result should be respected;[34] conscription was no longer a viable option. But NSW Labor's great reforming minister in education and local government would never return to elective office again.

On 6 November 1916, Labor's NSW General Secretary, Percy Charles Evans, wrote to certain MLAs to advise of their expulsions from the party for publicly advocating conscription or for standing with Mr Hughes on the conscription question. Those NSW MLAs who received their expulsion notices were: James Arkins,[35] MP for Castlereagh; William Ashford, MP for Liverpool Plains, Minister for Lands; William Bagnall,[36] MP for St George; George Burgess,[37] MP for Burrangong; Thomas Crawford,[38] MP for Marrickville; Alfred Edden,[39] MP for Kahibah; Arthur Gardiner,[40] MP for Newcastle; Arthur Griffith; David Hall, MP for Enmore, Attorney-General and Minister for Justice; Robert Hollis,[41] MP for Newtown; William Holman, MP for Cootamundra and Premier; Henry Hoyle, MP for Surry Hills & Minister for Mines and Labour and Industry; James McGowen, MP for Redfern, Labor's first NSW Premier, 1910-1913; Richard Meagher, MP for Phillip and the Speaker in the NSW parliament; James Mercer,[42] MP for Rozelle; James Morrish,[43] MP for King; John Nicholson,[44] MP for Wollongong; Robert Scobie,[45] MP for Murray.

Watson was in the process of being expelled from his local Labor Branch, in Paddington. In early November 1916 a brief report in the *Sydney Morning Herald* noted Watson's role in the party he helped to found had ended abruptly: "Another protracted meeting of the executive of the PLL was held last evening, and among the matters considered was the attitude taken up by Mr J.C. Watson on the conscription issue. It was eventually resolved that Mr Watson's seat on the executive be declared vacant."[46] On 4 November 1916, the General Secretary of NSW Labor, P.C. Evans, wrote to Watson to say: "I am directed to officially intimate to you that owing to your refusal to conform with the Resolution passed by the Conference in reference to Conscription your position as a Member of the Executive is declared vacant."[47] Technically, this was not expulsion. It was removal of Watson's place on the executive, on which his active involvement had commenced a quarter of a century before.

The witch-burning was not over. Ironically, on the official stationery of Evans' letter to Watson was an advertisement for Labor propagandist, author, state MP and minister George Black's *History of the New South Wales Labor Party*. At this time, Black was weighing up what to do. Although moderately anti-conscription, Black respected Hughes' reasoning that he and the government faced the dilemma of how to re-energise Australia's contribution to win the war. He was opposed to the expulsions. And he ended up expelled himself[48] and seeking Nationalist endorsement in early 1917,[49] lamenting: "He was deeply hurt at recent events. The Movement had been to him a pillar of cloud by day/and pillar of fire by night, now it is a mirage by day and *ignis fatuus* [foolish flame or will-o'-wisp] by night. The Johnny-come-latelys, the extremists and the self-seekers had dashed out the brains of the Labor Movement on the steps of the Trades Hall and Macdonell House [headquarters of the AWU]."[50] Black resentfully referred to the first organised faction within NSW Labor, the 'Industrial Section' formed in 1915 which changed its name to the 'Industrial Vigilance Council' in 1918, a fiery combination of industrial militancy and left-sloganising which came to briefly rule the roost in NSW Labor to 1919.[51]

On 13 November 1916, writing to Lawrence O'Hara,[52] the Honorary Secretary of the Paddington PLL, Watson responded to an invitation to speak at a meeting convened for the 14th of that month "to show cause why I should not be expelled on account of my attitude on the question of conscription."[53] Watson noted his other pressing commitments, including a meeting of Directors of Labor Papers Limited, which precluded his attendance. He went on: "I may say at once that I cannot recognise the right of the Paddington League to expel me for advocating 'Yes' in the referendum." Watson explained:

> I have not broken any pledge in taking the action objected to, nor have I contravened any portion of the Labor plat-

form or rules of the PLL. The last State Conference certainly carried a resolution opposing conscription. But that only accounted to an expression of opinion on the part of the members and was in no way binding on members of the organisation generally.

Watson continued, arguing that only if the national Labor Platform was amended could he be said to be in breach. He ended his letter:

> If a majority of the League, without authority under its own constitution, decides to expel me from the movement which I helped to establish 25 years ago, and to the principles of which I have consistently been faithful during the intervening period, I can only say that such illegal action is more likely to injure than help the cause of Labor in the future.

Beazley characterised Watson's response "as a model of Party constitutional correctness and also of political unreality."[54] Watson, on this view, was too aloof from the brutal politics unfolding, the passions about regimentation of the populace. Yet surely Watson had a point: The Labor Cabinet and Caucus had endorsed Hughes' referendum. Watson believed that being expelled for a position not covered in the Labor Platform was unfair. As he said five months later: "In previous times ... Labor men, apart from the platform were as free as air,"[55] but no longer. "Once when a man pledged himself to the platform, he knew it could be relied on for three years, but now it could be altered at each PLC conference"[56] and be immediately binding on party members, depriving them of any right to seek to alter the platform.

On 6 January 1917 Hughes invited Win-the-War supporters to a meeting at the Melbourne Town Hall. Manning Clark concluded: "J.C. Watson... had wanted the words 'desirous of ensuring a progressive National Policy' in the letter of invitation. Hughes refused."[57] Perhaps Hughes did not want debate on what 'progressive' might mean and in the process antagonising potential conservative allies. On 9 January, the public meeting occurred, Watson in the chair.[58] Hughes had in mind the urgency of political stability and the presentation of a new party, the National Party, that would both win the war and serve future needs. After lengthy negotiations, on 17 February 1917 a new Nationalist government was formed. The Cabinet consisted of 5 National Labor members and 6 former Liberal Party members, among them Joseph Cook, the new Deputy Prime Minister, and Sir John Forrest, the new Treasurer.

Was the 1916 Labor split inevitable? The divergence between Hughes and many others of the older generation, usually moderate in their Labor politics and more often British-born, and a younger generation, more radical, more socialist-inclined, and more likely local-born, was one aspect of the divide. But as summaries of the lives of those expelled MPs suggests, tidy explanations and clear-cut characteristics of those who 'left' are elusive. Each case was personal and distinctive.

The split affected the state Labor parties in different ways. In Queensland, all but one of the Labor ministers opposed conscription, and Labor retained power with only one MLA's defection. On the other hand, in New South Wales all Labor ministers supported conscription bar one, and a coalition was established with the Liberals to form a local version of the Nationalist Party.

In 1917, Watson argued that he had not twisted; it was Labor that had reversed its previous position out of recognition: "He had not altered; it was the party that had done that, leaving him where he was before."[59] Watson might have thought a progressive, Nationalist Party could emerge from the ashes of old Labor. In early 1917, Watson was in the thick of organising activity. As noted, on 9 January 1917, he presided over a meeting at the Melbourne Town Hall to form the National Federation.[60] Described as its chairman, on returning to Sydney from a trip to Melbourne, Watson surmised "that the idea of a separate party, bent on carrying on the affairs of the nation successfully till the end of the war, seems to have been favourably received…" and he speculated that various bodies might affiliate with the new party organisation, without necessarily formally merging.⁶¹ But both National Labor and the Commonwealth Liberals decided to merge on 13 February 1917. Later that month, Watson presided over a meeting of the executive committee of the National Federation, with his old friend Hector Lamond appointed as one of two honorary secretaries.⁶²

The Nationalist Party of Australia won the May 1917 Federal election. The Nationalists became the main conservative party of Australia until 1931. The split resulted in many early Labor figures ending their careers on the same bench with conservative MPs. The political fallout from the referendum was immense. At the 1917 election held after the party blew 'its brains out', discarding many of the old Labor MPs, it is remarkable how well the Labor vote held up. The Nationalists scored 54.22% of the vote and Labor 43.94%. That election was the last Federal House of Representatives poll using the 'first past the post' ballot method. From 1919, Australia switched to the preferential voting system.

Table 2: Federal Elections and Representation Post the ALP Split of 1916/17

Party	1917 Votes %	1917 Seats[i]	1919 Votes %	1919 Seats[ii]	1922 Votes %	1922 Seats[iii]	1925 Votes %	1925 Seats[v]
Nationalists	54.22	53	45.62	37	35.23	26	42.46	37
Liberal Union	0	0	0	0	2.41	3		
Country Party	0	0	8.72	11	12.56	14	10.74	13
Independent	1.85	0	2.98	1	3.28	1	1.76	2
Labor	43.94	22	42.49	26	42.30	29[iv]	45.04	23[iv]
Industrial Socialist Labor	0	0	0.19	0				
Liberal					2.04	2		
Total of Voting MPs		75		75		75		75

Notes:

i) To 1918, the Commonwealth Franchise Act 1902 and the Commonwealth Electoral Act 1902 together provided for a secret ballot, votes for men and women (but not for aboriginals), and plurality ("first-past-the-post") voting for both the Senate and the House of Representatives.

ii) After 1918, consequent to amendments to the Commonwealth Electoral Act 1918 optional preferential voting was introduced for Australian House of Representatives elections.

iii) The Northern Territory gained non-voting representation in the House of Representatives from 1922.

iv) Labor won the NT seat; this was additional to the 75-voting members.

v) Compulsory voting introduced in 1924.

Table 3: NSW Elections and Representation Post the ALP Split of 1916/17

Party	1917 Votes %	1917 Seats	1920 Votes %	1920 Seats	1922 Votes %	1922 Seats	1925 Votes %	1925 Seats
Nationalist	47.44	53	29.92	28	43.17	41	36.26	32
Independent Nationalist	2.47	0	1.60	2	0	0	0.99	1
Progressive			15.12	15	11.05	9	9.10	9
Country Party								
Independent	4.14	3	4.38	1	4.66	2	3.11	1
Labor	42.63	33	43.08	43	38.48	36	47.85	46
Independent Labor	3.26	1	0	0	1.58	0		
Protestant Labor							2.55	1
Socialist Labor	0.06	0	1.06	1	0.19	0		
Democratic					1.70	1		
Independent Coalitionist					0.71	1		
Total		90		90		90		90

Notes: Colin A. Hughes, *Voting for the New South Wales Legislative Assembly, 1890-1964*, Research School of Social Sciences, ANU, Canberra, 1975.

10

WHY THE LABOR SPLIT WENT SO DEEP AND CONTINUED

Applying a version of Dornbusch's Law, adapted for ALP characteristics, as discussed in the opening chapter of this book, it can be seen that the Labor conscription split began like a warming Rotorua geothermal lake, heating up to geyser eruptions, and then unexpected molten rock explosions. The Labor conscriptionists saw themselves as principled and courageous in the contest for authority in the movement. Their opponents thought the same about themselves. It is doubtful that the former had any expectation that the rupture with colleagues would be so savage. Or that the consequences and rancour would be so long-lasting.

Watson's rhetoric, as noted in the previous chapter, tried to be respectful to opponents. But to no avail. Perhaps the only way a major split could have been avoided in 1916 was if Germany had surrendered and the Allies had a quick victory and divisions in Australian Labor might then have been papered over. But the Germans and the Central Powers were not so obliging. The continuation of the War, the loss of so many more in the trenches, the 'gaps' in volunteers needed, all propelled Hughes to put forward a further referendum. Circumstances, differences in perspective on compulsion, and cultural antagonisms combined to ensure enmities became deeper and, between the old labour movement pioneers and the 'new starts', more hateful.

In 1917 Britain sought a sixth Australian division for active service, requiring 7000 men per month to meet the request. Volunteer recruitment supposedly continued to lag and on 20 December 1917, Prime Minister Hughes put a second referendum to the Australian people. This time the referendum asked:

> Are you in favour of the proposal of the Commonwealth Government for reinforcing the Commonwealth Forces overseas?

Hughes' proposal tried to nod favourably to voluntary enlistment as well as to compulsion. Any shortfall would be met by compulsory reinforcements of single men, widowers, and divorcees without dependents, aged between 20 and 44 years, who would be called up by ballot. No one was in any doubt, however, about the consequence of a positive vote. It was conscription. The referendum was defeated with 1,015,159 in favour and 1,181,747 against.

Although the 1917 referendum question was more narrowly drawn and less far-reaching than the 1916 question, the anti-conscription vote won by a larger margin. The vote in each state and territory was less in favour than in 1917 with the single exception of South Australia (although a clear majority there was still opposed.) In 1917, only Western Australia and Tasmania voted in favour, with Victoria almost evenly split with a majority of a little over 7,000 against out of nearly 679,000 voters. NSW voted nearly 59.0% against.

The conscription referenda were divisive politically, socially, and religiously. Newspapers and magazines of the time highlight the arguments, doubts, turmoil, and passion of Australians in debating and deciding the issue. The decisive defeat of the second referendum finished the issue of conscription for the remainder of the War.

Internationally, a turning point was the United States entering the fray, declaring war on Germany in April 1917, then on the Austro-Hungarian Empire in December 1917, and committing troops, treasure, and resources to boost the Allies. They turned a stalemate into victory. On the eleventh hour of the eleventh day of the eleventh month, Greenwich-mean-time, 11 November 1918, an armistice came into effect. In four years of war, more than 420,000 Australians volunteered for the AIF, the Navy and the Nursing Corps, and 60,000 of them died for their country.

At the 13 December 1919 Federal election, the two major parties were more evenly matched, 45.62% for the Nationalists and 42.49% for Labor. This election was held to capitalise on the popularity of Hughes after his return from the Paris Peace Conference.

In 1920, Holman was defeated in NSW elections by a revitalised Labor. Although the Storey Labor government was dissected and characterised by the Marxist-dreamer-scholar, Vere Gordon Childe,[1] as lacking in socialist ardour, Watson must have seen shadows and reminders of what he fought for: pragmatic, solid, sensible Labor trying to better the lives of its people. Labor in 1920, however, stood in contrast to the mostly harmonious workings of party administration in Watson's heyday. He saw a movement torn by convulsions and 'conflicts of disloyalties'[2] unlike anything he could remember.

On 16 December 1922, Federal elections were held, and Labor became the single largest party, Hughes only retaining the prime ministership with the support of the Country Party. Representation of the Nationalists was halved compared to 1917 and only a few of those left after 1922 in the House of Representatives were from Hughes' ex-Labor ranks. It was a similar story in NSW. Hagan and Turner point out: "After the 1920 [NSW] elections, only three Holmanites would remain in the Assembly, and Holman was not one of them."[3]

It appears from the early 1920s that Watson drifted away from active party-political engagement, though there were reports that he was concerned about the ALP socialist objective debate in 1921.[4] In the main, his life turned to business interests. As the President of the National Roads and Motorists Association (NRMA) from 1920, and later as chair of Australian Motorists Petroleum and Oil Limited (Ampol) from 1936, he needed to get on with all sides of politics. For this, he needed to be the wise statesman, respected and not too controversial, certainly not an aggravating enemy of anyone politically prominent. That had been his life, his reputation, right up to his expulsion from the party in 1916.

Watson insisted he was still true to Labor ideals. To an interjection in April 1917 at a public rally that he had joined the conservatives, Watson snapped back: "For the war only – the war is paramount"[5] and criticised the "No" voting Tudorites – Frank Tudor MHR[6] was then the Leader of the Opposition and Labor's national Leader – for not joining a government of all the parties, a national unity government, as had occurred in the UK.

While the most hardline positions were not those of the mainstream Labor leadership or that of most party members, in the immediacy of the Great Labor Split on conscription, the hardliners could subliminally shape moderate left values — and the views of progressive voters who followed or accepted the wider canon as to 'what people like me think'. In Victorian Labor politics, for example, the most hardline anti-conscriptionists were often the angriest capitalism sceptics, the 'we have no dog in this fight' minimisers about the War, and those most committed to attacks on the ruling elite. It was 'them versus us' outsider politics, which narrowed Labor's appeal.

How did this matter? All movements have core beliefs. The answer is that the culture of dissent became more intolerant, the package of ideas and feelings shifted. With so many politicians expelled or leaving the ALP, the freedom of conscience tolerated on some issues was replaced with a more rigid caucusing of MPs. This silenced scepticism and narrowed the Labor party — sometimes to the point of hounding out dissenters. This theme infuses Evatt's regretful account of Holman's expulsion and its legacy.[7] Some of the new faction leaders imagined Labor MPs as like gundogs bringing a rabbit or a bird to their master. Despite his service to the party Evans, for example, the former NSW Labor General Secretary who told Watson he was 'out', was himself summarily expelled in January 1920 after he fell out with Bailey, the AWU leader.[8] With his preselection as candidate for Goulburn withdrawn in favour of Bailey – who needed a new seat after a redistribution – Evans "decided to come out and fight his traducers and, if possible, to overthrow machine politics, which were the curse of the country."⁹ It was a bit too late by then. Labor's factional wars were most intense in NSW and lasted to the end of the 1930s.[10]

A less broad church became self-perpetuating. This is because activists select candidates in their own image. Factional leaders pick acolytes and others they think they can control. Moderate party members and broader-minded political leaders had to fight the narrowing current. In NSW, the traducing and expulsion of opponents reached embarrassing extremes. Factional self-interest, taking the spoils, masqueraded as stances of high principle. In the extreme, opponents were dehumanised, and politicians pulled away from the moderation and compromise that intractable problems generally require. Hence Anstey's prominence immediately during and after the conscription fight, and his popular, simple-minded ideas on the "money power".[11]

Rawson describes the organisational development of the ALP between 1916 and 1941, as lying between two great periods of parliamentary success. Few Labor achievements, however, marked the intervening twenty-five years. Except in Queensland where Labor governed in the whole period but for one term, state Labor governments were usually of short duration and frequently ended in disruption and disaster. Yet it was not an era of unqualified decline, for at its conclusion the party was able to begin a fruitful period of political supremacy.[12]

The political crisis in 1916 ultimately forced Laborites to choose between traditions, leaders, and competing narratives. The conflicts involved led pro-War politicians like James Catts, who wanted more troops through voluntary recruitment, uncertain at first as to what to say and do about more leftward stances, while those like Watson, whose affections and identity lay with the Empire and living up to the promise of "the last man and last shilling" for the War, wept for the destruction of a once coherent and compelling case for Labor.

What Watson had helped to build survived the storm and his own disillusionment. Eventually, Labor politics calmed down. The former young firebrand, William "Bill" McKell, won leadership of the NSW ALP in 1939, replacing the divisive Jack Lang, and was elected Premier on 16 May 1941. Another responsible radical, John Curtin, won Federal ALP leadership on 1 October 1935 and became Prime Minister on 7 October 1941. In 'the McKell Labor model' Watson could see echoes of his younger self, a style of moderate, progressive Labor politics. In thinking about the intervening period, from the tearing apart of Labor unity in 1916 to the day of Watson's death on 18 November 1941, the old Irish quip about the best way to reach a destination comes to mind: "I wouldn't start from here."

11

Business Life

I

Immediately after leaving parliament, Watson explored multiple business opportunities. There was no parliamentary pension in those days. He was not wealthy and needed work. Getting rich quickly as an ambition receded to a steady mission of gradual improvement.

At the risk of audacious thieving, Max Weber's lines about 'Politics as a Vocation' and his insistence that: "Politics is a strong and slow boring of hard boards", can be adapted to a particular business frame, which was Watson's chief focus for the bulk of his business career:

> It takes both passion and perspective. Certainly, all historical experience confirms the truth – that man would not have attained the possible unless time and again he had reached out for the impossible. But to do that a man must be a leader, and not only a leader but a hero as well, in a very sober sense of the word. And even those who are neither leaders nor heroes must arm themselves with that steadfastness of heart which can brave even the crumbling of all hopes. This is necessary right now, or else men will not be able to attain even that which is possible today.[1]

Politics, the small-p version, is more than what politicians do. Reaching out for the impossible, in Weber's phrase, as much as the persistent dedication to gradual betterment, are political activities. This idea has wide application to the mediation, resolution, and contest for resources, policies, and interests, in business as much as other places. In the concluding phase of his life, Watson's political skills, what he learnt through failure and success, experimentation, stumbles, and leadership, came to the fore. He never ceased learning. Mistakes and innovation are two handshakes of creative endeavour.

Reducing the former without fearsomely retiring to quietude and excessive caution, is the art of deftly growing business expertise.

Watson turned first to gold mining, then company director roles and, most significantly and long-lastingly, became the public face and President of a national motorists' organisation. Along the way, he met men who turned into mentors then business colleagues, as he developed a flair for enterprise and commercial adroitness.

As earlier noted, in 1910, the man who had been Prime Minister of Australia was at age 43 still a prospector and organiser of gold mining in South Africa, associated with Melbourne businessman and mining entrepreneur, William Tewksbury. Ellis notes:

> Anybody seeing the photograph [see p. 73 of this book] of the tall, beardless athletic figure in leggings photographed between two naked little black Africans beside a kraal at the Rondavels in the Transvaal[2] in 1910 would have been hard put to it to recognise the bearded, open-faced Prime Minister of 1904. He had receded into another world without regrets and without any ambition to return.[3]

Ironically, there was contemporary press and public criticism of Watson employing black labour in South Africa, instead of exclusively white labour. For example, Sir Joseph Carruthers scolded: "The Labor party talks a great deal about a White Australia, but when Mr. Watson went to South Africa, he did not hesitate to employ black labour. I do not say he was wrong, but the expressed views of Mr. Watson in Australia are not in harmony with the acts of Mr. Watson as a mine-owner in South Africa."[4] This comment was highly politically charged, published on the day of the 1910 Federal election.

In 1910-11, Watson extricated himself from the failed South African gold mining dredging venture, which besides Tewksbury as a stakeholder in the 'original syndicate' included "a number of members of the Federal Parliament."[5] Earlier indications from drilling and mine shafts were not reflective of potential. Watson explained: "Yes, it is one of those bits of bad luck that will always happen, and one cannot help."[6] In exiting that business, Watson earnt Tewksbury's respect, a man who, interestingly, later plied his skills at various motoring and taxi-related businesses.[7]

Fred William Hughes (no relation to W.M.), pastoralist and industrialist, became Watson's friend, another mentor. Watson joined the boards of his wool scouring, spinning, and textile businesses. This was mostly away from the glare of the public eye. The Great Depression in the early 1930s, however, found Watson, the company director and businessman, awkwardly rubbing shoulders with the union movement. He was then a Director of Alexandria Spinning Mills and H.W. Hughes Pty Ltd.

Watson was sometimes engaged as an independent arbitrator to solve commercial and industrial relations disputes. He chaired a pro-Protection industry lobby. One reason to throw himself ever deeper into business activities came after his wife Ada died of complications from influenza in July 1921.[8]

As noted earlier, on 30 October 1925 Watson married 23-year-old Western Australian, Antonia Mary Gladys Dowlan.[9] They headed off on a motoring honeymoon[10] and later had one child, a daughter, Jacqueline.

Of Watson's involvement in the NRMA, Ellis says Watson's "association with Tewksbury a motoring pioneer had started him on this course."[11] Though not much is known about how this friendship led to the NSW post, some facts are clear.

II

In a 1929 *Smith's Weekly* profile, the cliched tribute "king of the roads" was used, though the author perceptively said that in reaching that mark of prominence, it was "not that [Watson] was conspicuous among motorists; not that he hankered any longer after a place of political importance, but only that he was a tireless man who must fit himself into work of real organisation somewhere or other." The appointment followed Sir Owen Cox's withdrawal[12] as

MISS ADELINA LANE, whose marriage with Mr. J. C. Watson, first Labor Prime Minister of Australia, took place in Sydney on Saturday.

MRS. J. C. WATSON, wife of the first Labor Prime Minister of Australia, who was Miss Antonia Lane. — (Monte Luke photo.)

Mrs J.C. Watson, *The Daily Telegraph* [Sydney, NSW], 17 October 1925, p. 2 and Wedding photo News, *The Sun News Pictorial* [Melbourne, Victoria] 7 October 1925, p. 11. Both articles mistakenly refer to Antonia Dowlan as Adelina Lane.

inaugural president of the National Roads Association (NRA) in 1920, replaced by Watson from 16 August 1920.[13] The NRA set for itself the task to lobby for "reasonable and just legislation" to fund and improve roads. The organisation was renamed the National Roads' and Motorists' Association (NRMA) in January 1924. Then as now, the NRMA is an Australian member-owned mutual company limited by guarantee.

The arrival of motorised road transport in Australia in the early part of the twentieth century promised excitement, speed, convenience, the feeling of freedom, and danger. The mass production of the 1908 Ford Model T revolutionised motor vehicle deployment across the world, including Australia.[14] Middle-class everyman, not

THE PRESIDENT'S MESSAGE

(The Hon. J. C. Watson, ex-Prime Minister of the Commonwealth.)

In launching the "Good Roads Magazine" the National Roads Association hopes to further stimulate public interest in the all-important question of improving our national Highways. Broadly speaking, the condition of its roads has for centuries been accepted as the measure of a nation's progress. When "all roads led to Rome" the engineers had accomplished more for the

civilisation of that day than had Rome's greatest military leaders. To-day, as ever, cheap transport still largely depends upon the cost of road traction.

Where real roads have been laid down and (which is just as important) maintained, as in the Eastern States of America, the latest development is to rely solely upon road transit for the shorter hauls. Easy haulage reflects itself in reduced cost of transport, whether the vehicle be horse-drawn or motor-propelled. Reduced transport charges mean cheaper commodities, and therefore every citizen is vitally interested in good roads.

The National Roads Association has endeavoured to demonstrate the value of good roads, but although something has been achieved the response is still insufficient. Individuals will gather together and discuss the disgraceful condition of the roads hour after hour, and yet you will usually find that these men are not even members of the Association. Every other country has demonstrated the value of good roads, and the advantages to be gained are so obvious that it is extraordinary that this subject is not more fully appreciated. Good Roads mean to the farmer an increased marketing radius and a decreased cost of production. Similarly it means a reduction in the high cost of living, and in these troublous times this objective is most desirable.

No more striking example could be afforded than that of the Parramatta Road. As early as 1854 questions were asked in the House of Parliament as to when the Parramatta Road would be repaired, and that question has been brought up year after year until the Parramatta Road was the laughing stock of the whole Commonwealth. It is no exaggeration to say that recently in wet weather it was absolutely impassable, and this within a radius of 7 miles from Sydney.

Fortunately the Government in power at the present time devoted to the roads question a consideration which had never previously been bestowed on it, and determined to repair the Parramatta Road immediately. Thirteen Councils were involved in the control of the road, and it is common knowledge that some of these Councils refused even to co-operate with the Government in repairing the road.

The Government, despite these obstacles, repaired the Parramatta Road, and to-day the property values along that road have increased enormously, and Parramatta is now within 50 minutes travel of the city. The same analogy applies to the roads throughout the whole of this State. There are 97,399 miles of roads in the State of New South Wales, and of this total only 18,612 miles are gravelled, metalled or more highly improved. Is not that sufficient justification for the existence of the National Roads Association?

The Council trusts that members will give the "Good Roads Magazine" hearty support in its effort to energize the public on this matter. We want every far-sighted citizen to join the Good Roads Association and help to sweep aside the apathy now prevailing. With additional membership we can present to the authorities an irresistible demand that the roads of the State should be put in order.

J. C. WATSON.

AFTER READING PASS "GOOD ROADS" ON TO INTERESTED FRIENDS.

Watson in NRMA publications wrote numerous articles updating members of campaigns and efforts by his officers to persuade governments to better target road and safety improvements. This one is from 1921.

only the rich, became the market, though there were years ahead before that potential was realised. Upton Sinclair's 1927 novel *Oil!* extols individualistic *joi de vivre* of driving on an open stretch of road:

> The road ran, smooth and flawless, precisely fourteen feet wide, the edges trimmed as if by shears, a ribbon of grey concrete, rolled out over the valley by a giant hand. The ground went in long waves, a slow ascent and then a sudden dip; you climbed, and went swiftly over – but you had no fear, for you knew the magic ribbon would be there, clear of obstructions, unmarred by bump or scar, waiting the passage of inflated rubber wheels revolving seven times a second ... you sat snug behind a tilted wind-shield, which slid the gale up over your head.[15]

It took foresight to imagine and exploit the opportunities that were opening. From its formation in 1903, the Royal Automobile Club of Australia (RACA) also campaigned for better roads. The club's Good Roads Association, formed in 1912, was a manifestation of that – attracting support from the *Sydney Morning Herald* and regional newspapers. Of itself, this indicated the growing, persistent constituency of motorists wanting governments to do better. The NRA saw a gap in what the genteel officeholders of the RACA could offer – though at first there was a personnel overlap of directors in both bodies. The NRA aimed to become a broader and stronger pressure group with comparable objectives to the RACA, with support from the latter. The new body embarked on an imaginative programme of practical work.

Watson led the NRMA until his death in 1941. The aims of the NRMA were to "cover everything necessary for the advancement and protection of motorists in all circumstances," barely different from the RACA's. Both had an eye on the government purse to fund improved road networks, repairs and maintenance. Both were competitors and collaborators, sometimes uneasily so; one was to eclipse the other. Merger discussions were resisted by the NRMA, which had outgrown its sister body.[16] By 1946, the RACA ceased its rival

Old Dog for Hard Road, *Sunday Times* [Sydney, NSW], 15 January 1928, p. 3.

road service operations in favour of the NRMA. There is no doubt that Watson made a large difference in the NRMA easily surpassing its older cousin.

In a colourful 1937 profile in *The Sun* newspaper, Watson was called "a sort of unofficial PM of Auto-Australia", another stale phrase, with the writer in a livelier mood saying:

Discarded politicians, battling 'on the outer' for a possible Restoration, are a sorry spectacle. Mr. Watson was not discarded; he stepped out of high place of his own accord. He linked himself at length with the woolly interests of F.W. Hughes, and then became the public advocate of motorists as head serang in the NRMA.[17]

That was an interesting insight, repeated in a plethora of profiles and articles about Watson in his lifetime. He exuded the image of the quintessential, reasonable man.

Jim Russell's sketch of Watson, *Smith's Weekly* [Sydney], 23 June 1934, p. 4.

Why was Watson considered suitable for the roads' body? An interest in policy development, commercial astuteness, fair-mindedness, uprightness, and decency were key characteristics to lead a fledging lobby group that aimed to be a substantial force in the land. Knowing 'who-is-who in the zoo', as the expression goes, mattered, as did the ability to command respect to open doors, get an audience with key people, decision-makers in politics and the bureaucracy. Media savvy, understanding how to crisply present a story in clear language, 'knowing what buttons to press' were desirable too. A grasp of economics, of budgets and 'value for money', and an appreciation of costs and benefits, complete the ideal resume.

Such features made Watson an attuned President of the National Roads and Motorists Association (NRMA). A detailed story (more than can be recounted here) ought to be written about how Watson went about that business, arguing for motorists, pressing governments and bureaucrats for attention, seeking increased spending commitments in government budgets, local, state, and national.

To be effective, Watson had to be strategic – focused on services to build scale and rapport with motorists, raising road safety as an objectively important priority - and tactical - such as pressuring governments on the worthiness of particular road projects. Sometimes both aspects were combined in presenting and prosecuting points, a combination of niggling, needling, cajoling, and bellowing.

In the relentless pursuit of 'more' for the motorist, better roads, cheaper petrol,[18] quality cars, lower taxes, it helped that Watson thought what he was asking for was representative of what the man and woman 'behind the wheel' would want.

The NRMA became a consumer watchdog, an insurance broker turned insurer, the motorist's friend through all its services including extensive roadside assistance, and the ranking and giving the NRMA 'stamp of approval' to authorised, independent dealers as well as mechanical repair shops: "Everybody who has ever put his foot on the gas knows the road reports and the road maps of the

NRMA, its service stations, its technical and legal advices, and the benefits of its insurance."[19] The organisation became the essential adjunct to owning or leasing a car. Watson's country background (his MP life started as the MLA for Young in the NSW parliament), his political reach over decades, was handy. He knew residents in regional areas. The folk 'in the bush' were often resentful that city folk had better and closer access to the decision-makers in town. This meant that the NRMA had to speak credibly for them too, not only for city drivers. Watson foresaw that motor vehicles were key to the development of regional areas through 'motor touring' much along the lines described in Sinclair's *Oil!* Through the NRMA's *Open Road* magazine, motoring holidays were promoted.

Yet, although "… the N.R.M.A. developed into a powerful economic unit, with a press and propaganda and policy of its own" it never "succeeded in cutting back the petrol tax," once it was introduced.[20] Watson was concerned both about petrol companies profiteering, "amassing vast sums from Australian motor users"[21] as well as petrol duties/taxes on petrol charged by the government, which kept going up.[22] Watson had a broad remit as the public face of advocacy for motorists. In 1933 he appeared before the NSW Royal Commission on petrol prices. As a representative of consumers, Watson said he feared "for the outcome of the petrol war now raging."[23]

In 1935 a consortium of New Zealand businessmen backed Arthur O'Callaghan, George Walkley, and George Hutchison of the Automobile Association of Auckland, New Zealand, when they approached the NRMA in Sydney offering to repeat a New Zealand experiment in forming a company to compete with the overseas oil companies to drive down prices. Those businessmen suggested to the NRMA that they form an Australian company to market petrol in response to concerns about inequitable petrol pricing and transfer pricing by foreign oil companies. Broomham says: "Watson favoured direct involvement but [the NRMA] Council [in 1935] harboured grave doubts about the company's ability to prevail against entrenched oil interests."²⁴ Dyster notes: "The price of petrol, and alleged transfer pricing to limit the tax foreign oil companies paid, were also bitter issues in Australia. The NRMA council decided not to sponsor an oil company officially, but its president, Chris Watson, and its secretary, treasurer and solicitors sought investors."²⁵ The Australian Motorists' Petrol Association company's formation was mooted in early 1936, noting that a similar company had been established in New Zealand. Watson is referred to: "His association with the company is taken to mean that the new organisation intends to market petrol at a price lower than the existing rate."²⁶ On 23 March 1936, the Australian Motorists Petrol Company was incorporated in New South Wales. Early in 1936 the *Open Road*, the NRMA's periodical, publicised the float of the Australian Motorists Petroleum Co. Ltd.²⁷ and Watson became the Chair of the Ampol Board. It was the first oil company in which the Australian public could buy shares. In 1939, Walkley joined the Ampol Board as Managing Director.²⁸

The first decades after the T-model and other inventive motor vehicle improvements, with gleaming machines rolling off production lines, meant that Sinclair's words in *Oil!* and the exuberance of industry bodies like the NRMA about motoring tourism rehearsed "the inventory of metaphors that the road and motoring [bodies] were germinating for bourgeois sociality in the 1920s. Metaphors of efficiency, rationalisation, [conveyed] the collective sense of an individualism realised at the wheel …"²⁹ Such giddy tributes and endorsements also reflected part of the lived experience of members of the public.

More innovation came when in the 1920s the NRMA employed road service 'guides' who, at the beginning, were mostly returned servicemen "of exemplary character" who patrolled specific areas at congested spots on the roads in and out of the city where they could receive messages by phone or relayed by other motorists.³⁰

In 1924-1925, the NRMA's membership doubled to 7,637 mem-

GOOD ROADS.
MOTORS AND THEIR CARE.

Mechanical First Aid—What to do until you get your Car to the Garage.
(By Easy-Running.)

[Motorists are asked to write for free advice about the running of their cars, where to get the best service, information re traffic regulations, etc. Address all enquiries to "Easy Running," c/o N.R.M.A. 30 Grosvenor Street, City. Enclose 1½d. stamp if a personal reply is required; otherwise it will be answered in this column each month.]

Four Wheel Brakes.

Motorists fitted with two wheel brakes should remember that a car fitted with four wheel brakes, travelling at the same rate as themselves, can pull up in a much shorter distance. Therefore, when in traffic or queues, ascertain if the car ahead of you is fitted with them, and act accordingly.

Petrol Filters.

All filters in your petrol system should be kept clean. More trouble is caused through dirty filters than any other single cause. The filters should be cleaned before taking any long run, and at least once a month if the car is used for city work.

You can ascertain where your filters are situated by glancing at your car's handbook. Usually one is to be found where the main petrol supply enters the vacuum tank, and another in the carburettor.

Of course some petrol contains more dirt, which would necessitate more attention.

Distilled Water.

Always keep the distilled water in your batteries well over the plates. If this is not done, your self-starter will fail, then your horn and then your lights. Also corrosion will set up in the plates, and your battery will be damaged. Therefore always carry a bottle of distilled water in your car. Procured at all chemists.
(See also page 28.)

REPAIRS WHILE YOU WAIT.—Guides rendering Mechanical First Aid to Motor Car.

One of many articles in NRMA publications promoting the services offered by the organisation to motorists. This one was published in 1924.

bers. In 1924, the NRMA decided to form NRMA Insurance and examined a relationship with Lloyd's of London, the insurance brokers, as a sub-agency with the aim to extend coverage to household policies as well as motoring insurance. In 1925, the Insurance Branch was set up, initially with no fresh capital – but with personal bank guarantees from twenty leading members including Watson.[31] Commissions were cut out, and an immediate reduction of 20 per cent in premiums effected. The bank guarantors were never called upon; there was never an overdraft.

In 1928, it was stated: "[w]hen Mr Watson became President of the NRMA in 1920, it only had a few hundred members. Today membership has reached 40,000."[32] In 1928, the Bavin government appointed Watson as Chairman of a Commission to investigate Sydney's traffic problems. A profile in the *Sunday Times* newspaper noted: "Nowadays, Mr Watson devotes most of his time to the NRMA" and lauded his role in making the organisation "one of the most modern self-help institutions in the world."[33]

By 1939 with 66,234 members, the NRMA had a sizable road service operation. During World War II, their force of 500 owner-drivers sometimes provided rapid troop transport. The NRMA Women's Auxiliary Transport Corps trained 506 women to handle trucks, lorries, ambulances, and motorcycles. In 1939-1941 and for the duration of World War II, the NRMA fostered information campaigns, including the discouragement of petrol hoarding, considered both unpatriotic and dangerous.

Watson was alert to the paradox of a politically active organisation eschewing partisan politics. Backing "the wrong horse" at an election would undermine the Association's effectiveness; appearing to be too cosy or partial to one political party would not be effective in the long-term. In 1930, Watson wrote: "The Association's political neutrality has earned it the respect of every Government, and it also probably explains why its sustained membership of 50,000 embraces every possible shade in the political spectrum."[34]

Watson greets Tewksbury at the Opening of the Yellow Cabs Sydney headquarters, *Evening News* [Sydney, NSW], 18 December 1925, p. 1.

For Watson, business was not a sad end to an accomplished career. He left politics of his own accord, "to work his own plough,"[35] as he once said. Everything he did in his earlier life was preparation for what was to come.

LABOR'S FIRST PRIME MINISTER

Motorists Lose their Keenest Champion with the Death of Hon. J. C. Watson

The NRMA magazine in November 1941 reports the death of Watson.

Photo of J.C. Watson, nd, J.C. Watson Papers, MS 451/8/ various photos, NLA.

12

Concluding Observations

Watson was present at the creation of the Australian Labor Party, when the unions revived in the early 1890s; when the party was formed in 1890, he was an active campaigner at the 1891 election when, at its first showing Labor won 35 seats in the NSW parliament; he chaired Labor's formative Solidarity Conference in 1893 which worked out the pledge and its subsequent iteration at the 1894 Conference; he won election and served for almost seven years in the NSW parliament, representing the rural electorate of Young; he won the seat of Bland for Labor as a member in the first Federal Parliament; he was selected to lead the new national party in 1901, becoming Prime Minister and Treasurer for 113 days in 1904, consistently doing better in votes and seats in leading Labor at the 16 December 1903 poll and the 12 December 1906 national election.

Throughout his leadership, 1901-1907, he had the reputation of "Yes, Mr Watson", as his Labor MPs mostly made the difference in deciding on contentious legislation and the formation of a government. The Labor bloc held the same power in the NSW parliament when Watson served. He guided and intervened in Labor party debates in NSW. And, especially, at the 1905, 1908, 1910 and 1914 national conferences, he helped shape policy on defence, pensions, arbitration, and other important platform items. He was active as an NSW Labor executive member, President, and sometimes acting President, through to the outbreak of the Great War.

With the Great Labor Split of 1916, everything changed. More than anyone else in its early years at the national level, Watson exemplified what Labor stood for, how it distinguished itself from opponents, what its platform should extol, and what should be rejected. He had to work out for himself and his colleagues how to deal with contentious questions centring on socialism, the resolution of strikes, land tax, the arbitration of industrial disputes, and expanded Commonwealth powers. They were matters he sometimes refereed on the playing field. Sometimes Watson ran onto the field of play to forcefully press his case. On his reckoning, middle of the road reforms, gradual improvements to society, were the substance of what realistically Labor could achieve. This was confidence in the inevitability of gradualness.

To say he was present at the formation and evolution of all this risks implying that Watson was merely present, roll-called, instead of at the core – completely in the thick of the creation — pleading, initiating, enlisting allies, rewriting draft motions, urging a speaker at a critical moment to get up and speak their mind, intervening himself in debates. Watson led the life of a leading political activist and Labor Party leader.

When the Labor tree shook free of pro-conscriptionists, of those pro-Empire loyalists who subscribed to the arguments of Hughes for compulsory military service, it was not as if falling leaves gently wafted and circled to the ground. Whole limbs of the tree were sawn- and torn- off. There was nothing gentle about the fall. It must have been an awful shock. Labor men (mostly) and women (some), comrades in so many political contests over time, were now ranged against each other.

It is hard to imagine any other person splitting the Labor Party in 1916 like Hughes. His predecessor as Prime Minister, Andrew Fisher, could never be persuaded to endorse compulsion, despite exhortation from his successor, including pleas when Fisher was Australia's High Commissioner in London, from January 1916 to January 1921. Smarting like Stan Laurel, Hughes did not put the effort into winning his own party to the course he believed. This was distinctly un-Watson-like.

Hughes had a tin ear. Away overseas from January to July 1916, he badly under-estimated how much ill-feeling was brewing on conscription. Hughes was let down by Senator George Foster Pearce, the Deputy Labor Leader and Defence Minister, and other colleagues, in their under-estimation of internal party opposition.

As Labor split wide open on the issue, Hughes and his most trusted ministers believed the loss of so many men in the battles at the Somme (1916) required urgent and significant replenishment. Compulsion, so that every man could play his part in the sacrifice, came to be Hughes' answer to pleas from the Imperial War Office for more men. That was Watson's view too. It would be a mistake, 120-years later, to see this as cringing subservience to the British Crown. As one summation of Australian British colonial outlook put matters: "What we are dealing with here is an Australia that saw itself, in cultural terms, not as colonial but as confidently provincial, standing in the same relationship to London as the great provincial cities of England."[1] Australians saw themselves as distinctly British, with interests that needed articulation and defending. As a British Australian, Watson believed that in difficult circumstances every able man had a duty to fight and, for the greater good, government should enforce and compel that duty.

This clarifying ambition was clouded by a raucous reaction. What was promised in earlier debates within Labor, compulsory training but no forcible conscription, a volunteer army, no compulsory sending of troops overseas, now clashed with Hughes' and Watson's view of what Australia needed to do to honourably discharge its obligations to the British Empire. A fantastic confidence about the course chosen defined Hughes. There were clever, well-meaning Laborites who urged Hughes to run on his record and help win the War with conscription, following what the United Kingdom (except for Ireland) and New Zealand did through legislation earlier in 1916. According to those enthusiasts, this Prime Minister was Australia's first notable leader on the world stage, a courageous war-time strategist, whose reforms and leadership back home, in the Fisher government, and through his own administration, merited more than appreciation – they commanded admiration. Yet the mood of the electorate was wary about compulsory overseas military service. Hughes' solution? The recourse of doomed strategies everywhere: to seek to communicate better, rather than revisiting the proposal on offer.

This led to targeted, tactical public relations hysteria. It meant not creatively and intelligently engaging opposing views. The self-righteous conclusion that your cause is obviously correct leaves little room to negotiate with others, let alone entertain doubt on first-order strategic principles. On this perspective, negotiation would contaminate the purity of what was espoused.

Even when Labor senators in September 1916 mostly broke on the vote to authorise a referendum, the Bill only passing with Opposition Senators' support, the calculation was that a sweeping referendum win would be its own justification, with reconciliation within Labor ranks possible thereafter. It was not to be. The populace on 28 October 1916 narrowly voted conscription down, invigorating Hughes' opponents within Labor, now inflamed by a resoundingly clear majority, and ensuring the split remained forever. Hughes and others were demonised. Watson, who barracked for Hughes' position, was spared the humiliation of the central executive expelling him. His local party branch did the deed. Perhaps alone of anyone significant on the 'Yes' side, Watson was given the chance to recant after the referendum vote in late October. He did not. Watson's branch, too, was thrown into the fire. He was expelled from the party he loved. Shouting back at the gobbling flames made no difference.

The 'Labor conscriptionists', the National Labor Party, to use the term used at the end of 1916, were now isolated. Few seemed to realise that what had gone wrong was their basic proposition, not its framing or messaging.

Yet, in December 1917, with more losses and casualties on the Western Front, more recruitment problems, and the number of volunteers falling short of the 'ask', Hughes ran the conscription arguments again. Somewhat more subtly, but with no obscuring of the basic question, compulsion, was rehashed and served. Again, the referendum failed, this time by a bigger margin.

Hughes was out of his element at this level of politics. The moral question, dooming the unvolunteered to a conflict half a world away, was a fundamental problem, not a presentational snag. And there were the other potent arguments about training and mixing committed volunteers with 'cowardly' conscripts, and so forth.

The necessarily speculative question is whether Watson might have done better. Watson's conviction was to support Hughes, believing the need for more men overrode previous expressed scruples about conscription for the AIF. But Watson's style was not only to state a case but to listen to other points of view and craft a winning argument. It was all or nothing for Hughes. He always knew best, as if listening or revisiting or retreating was for weaklings. In contrast, as touched upon in the conscription chapter, Labor MHR Catts was for improving the efficiency and efficacy of recruitment efforts. But for Hughes the die was thrown. The first referendum result drove him and his supporters into a 'fight the war first' alliance that united into a single party prior to elections in May 1917, lest an awkwardly presented coalition appear unconvincing. Fused into one, into the Nationalist Party, were the National Labor and Liberal elements. Watson was helpful in its creation. But did the new party live up to the expectations of the old Labor people now in its ranks? The latter might have hoped for a future of progressive social legislation infused with Australian nationalist pride, a variant of Lib-Lab from the first decade of the century.

Hughes convincingly won the 1917 election in seats, and well, but not overwhelmingly, in votes. Arguably the roiling internal divisions in Labor thereafter kept most people from vigorously and hopefully knocking on Labor's door until it became safer to do so, many years later. Electorally Hughes' was successful into the early 1920s. Yet his biographer, Fitzhardinge, observes:

> Cut off from his political, social and even geographical roots, expelled by the party and the union which had been such a large part of his life, distrusted by his new supporters, he never, for all his public triumphs, regained the authority and confidence of his early days.[2]

We mostly do not know how Watson voted from the 1920s onwards, after Hughes was forced out of office by the Country Party, with the patrician Victorian, Stanley Melbourne Bruce, his replacement as Prime Minister in 1923. Notably though, Watson was reported in 1925 as supporting the Nationalist, Daniel Levy, as a state MP in NSW,[3] and he supported UAP leader Joe Lyons in 1931. Hughes was expelled by the Nationalists in 1929 after he led a revolt by dissidents over Bruce's failed radical reforms to abolish the Commonwealth Arbitration Court. Hughes marshalled the numbers to bring about his successor's defeat, an election followed, and Bruce was decisively defeated, losing his own seat.

On 31 October 1929 in Canberra, Watson made a friendly call on the new Prime Minister, James Scullin.[4] The *Australian Worker* noted the new Australian Prime Minister's many courtesy visits. "… Amongst those who dropped in was J.C. Watson, the first Labor Prime Minister of the Commonwealth. He was politely received, of course, for Jim Scullin is finely free of personal animosities, even though he fights with the gloves off in the political arena."[5] When Scullin visited Sydney in early December 1929, his first visit there as Prime Minister, Watson as President of the Australian Industries Protection League was one of various business leaders to greet him.[6]

The Scullin government collapsed under the weight of the Great Depression and the Lang attacks – a story told elsewhere.[7]

Into old age, Watson continued to devote himself to family, company directorships, and especially the NRMA, picking and choosing other interests, including serving as a Trustee of the Sydney Cricket Ground Trust (SCG),[8] playing golf,[9] joining the board of the Fellowship of Australian Writers, looking, according to one account in 1937, "a younger man with no beard. Mr. Watson looks a human being these days. So runs the latest post-mortem on an old Prime Minister."[10] Perhaps his healthy appearance was deceptive, as his health soon was in decline.

The SCG involvement is interesting. A vacancy on the SCG trust occurred in late 1914. Trustees suggested Watson as a potential replacement, and he was duly appointed by the NSW Holman Labor government and took his seat on 16 February 1915.[11] He "immediately requested five months' leave of absence, as he was due to leave for the United States and then Europe,"[12] including the UK. Rodney Cavalier notes:

> [Watson] was soon a key Trustee, often being part of deputations to government. He was regularly pressing for more capacity. One sees a pattern after [William] McKell's appointment in March 1931 of the duo working together. On 20 December 1938 Watson nominated McKell to the vacant position of Chairman. He was elected unopposed. There were no other obvious Labor voters among Trustees.[13]

Watson's time as a Trustee, a long-standing role he had sought, was an enjoyable part of his life, important to him.

Watson's death on 18 November 1941, aged 74, mellowed animosities from the Labor side. He had been unwell; he succumbed to cerebral thrombosis "after a four-year history of chronic myocarditis".[14] The words used in mourning and commemoration were so generous and consistent that the usual caution associated with 'never speaking ill of the dead' could not be the only explanation. They rang true and sincere. A friend from the days of yore, Arthur Griffith, wrote to Mrs Watson: "I have, during my long life, had many friends both personal and political but I have never known any more so entirely admirable and honourable, holding such high ideals and living up to them in his daily life."[15]

Watson's fears of the potential for Japan to menace Australian interests were dramatically accentuated in the months ahead. Pearl Harbour, "the day of infamy" in President Roosevelt's words, was bombed on 7 December 1941; Singapore fell on 15 February 1942;

and Darwin was bombed on 19 February 1942. But he did not live to see that.

The eight pallbearers at the funeral were Prime Minister, John Curtin; NSW Premier, William McKell; Federal leader of the United Australia Party, W.M. Hughes; former Prime Minister Sir Joseph Cook; former NSW Minister and ex-Federal MP David Hall; the President of the NSW Legislative Council Ernie Farrar;[16] the former NSW Minister Arthur Griffith; and former Senator Albert Gardiner.[17] All were current or former Labor MPs, the last six of whom, expelled or otherwise alienated from their old party, had known Watson well and worked closely with him in their earlier careers.[18] Ellis recalled:

> Many old, forgotten paladins of the early days of Labor whom one thought long dead appeared to see him off. Old Joseph Cook, 81 years old, who had been his colleague in the days of the foundation of the NSW Labor Party was there, beginning to quaver a little. He took my arm to steady himself as we walked out into the street afterwards. He remarked as one venerable colleague after another of the early days, now remote from the movement, came up to greet him: "It looks like the Day of Resurrection."[19]

McKell, as mentioned, got to know Watson through the SCG Trust and it is likely that they were friends. Curtin's role as a pallbearer was probably protocol. In the first half of the twentieth century, a tradition emerged of current or former Prime Ministers and Premiers, of whatever political persuasion, acting as pallbearers at funerals of a Prime Minister[20] and this continued in those more chivalrous times up to the mid-twentieth century.[21]

Watson's Labor DNA was passed on literally to his daughter, and the grandchildren he never knew, all of whom were sometime ALP members and/or supporters.[22]

More influentially, Watson's leadership was the standard for Labor in and out of government. But later others, Fisher, Curtin, Chifley, brought their distinct bearing, example, and leadership model to the role. Looking back, around 1914, Watson observed: "Starting essentially as a class party, and depending almost entirely upon artisans and manual labourers, it has gradually attracted wider support, until it now includes amongst its adherents a large portion of brain workers."[23]

Watson's own words, the finish to his 1914 manuscript on the Australian labour movement are apposite:

> No one can claim that success has attended all the Labor Party's efforts, but it may at least be said generally that it has advanced the cause of humanity by another step. It has taught the rank and file to know their strength and stressed the fact that the golden opportunities existent in Australia have never-ending responsibilities as their necessary accompaniment."[24]

Those words echo down the generations and sound a tocsin, a call to action, an insistence on responsibility too. That was very much how Watson saw the life of politics and service to his party, community, and the wider public.

Notes and Abbreviations

At the 1908 federal conference of the state parties, the name 'Australian Labor Party' was adopted for use. But it is useful to be aware that prior to and frequently thereafter, the individual parties retained their original names as adopted upon foundation. Thus:

NSW:	NSW: Political Labor League
Victoria:	Political Labor Council
Queensland:	Queensland Labour Party
South Australia:	United Labor Party
Western Australia:	Australian Labor Federation
Tasmania:	Tasmanian Workers' Political League

At the 1918 Federal Labor Conference in Perth, all agreed to adopt the same style. Hereafter they were titled Australian Labor Party (ALP), followed by the name of the state branch.

The state union federations, in contrast, retained their distinctive names and there was no consistency, even after the formation of the Australian Council of Trade Unions (ACTU) in 1927. Thus, in the relevant period covered here:

NSW:	Trades & Labor Council of Sydney, 1871-1894; the Sydney District of the Australasian Labour Federation, 1894-1900; the Sydney Labor Council, 1900-1908; Labor Council of New South Wales, after 1908.
Victoria:	Melbourne Trades Hall Committee (1856) known as the Victorian Trades Hall Council.
Queensland:	Brisbane Trades and Labor Council, 1885-1889; the Brisbane District Council of the Australasian Labor Federation, 1889-1914; the Brisbane Industrial Council, 1914-1917; The Trades and Labor Council of Queensland, 1922 onwards.
South Australia:	United Trades and Labour Council of South Australia

Western Australia:	The Trades & Labor Council, Perth (from 1891 to 1907) when it re-emerged as the Western Australian Branch of the Australian Labour Federation and in its leadership uniquely combined political Labor and industrial labour.
Tasmania:	Trades & Labor Council of Hobart, 1883-1917; Hobart Trades Hall Council, 1917-1968. (Only after 1968 were the separate Trades Halls of Hobart, Launceston and Devonport were amalgamated as the Tasmanian Trades & Labor Council.)

In this manuscript, in common with current usage, the one spelling of Australian Labor is used throughout, including in most quotes where 'Labour' is used. The *Sydney Morning Herald* persisted with spelling Labor with a 'u'. I removed that letter in most quotes from that source. In referencing the broader movement, "the Australian labour movement" term is usually deployed and, sometimes, Australian Labor Movement.

abt.	about
ACF	Australian Comfort Fund
ADB	Australian Dictionary of Biography
AIF	Australian Imperial Force
ALP	Australian Labor Party
Ampol	Australian Motorists Petroleum and Oil Limited
ANDL	Australian National Defence League
ANU	Australian National University
ANZAC	Australian and New Zealand Army Corps
Aotearoa	Māori-language name for New Zealand, "land of the long white cloud"
AWM	Australian War Memorial
AWU	Australian Workers' Union
Caucus	The Labor MPs meeting together in a parliament
CNZM	Companion of the New Zealand Order of Merit
fn.	footnote
ft.	foot (old imperial measurement)
Iss.	Issue
JCW	John Christian Watson

KBE	Knight Commander of the Most Excellent Order of the British Empire
MHR	Member of the House of Representatives
MLA	Member of the Legislative Assembly
MLC	Member of the Legislative Council
MP	Member of Parliament
MS	Manuscript
nd	Not dated
NAA	National Archives of Australia
NLA	National Library of Australia
NRA	National Roads Association
NRMA	National Roads and Motorists' Association
NSW	New South Wales
N.T.	Northern Territory, territory administered by the Australian government
NZ	New Zealand
pair	The arrangement between party whips for an absent member on one side to be "paired" with an absentee on the other.
Pakeha or Pākehā	Māori-language term for New Zealanders primarily of European descent
PLC	Political Labor Conference
PLL	Political Labor League
Qld	Queensland
RACA	Royal Automobile Club of Australia
RMS	Roads and Maritime Services
RTA	Roads and Traffic Authority
SA	South Australia
SCG	Sydney Cricket Ground Trust
SL	State Library
Snr	Senior
SS	Screw Steamer, i.e., a term for a steamship or steamboat powered by a steam engine, using one or more propellers (known as screws) to propel it through the water.
Tas	Tasmania, Australian state
TU	Trade Union

UAP	United Australia Party, i.e., the main anti-Labor party founded in 1931, formed from the Nationalist Party, the Lyons breakaway from Labor, and W.M. Hughes' Australia Party
UK	United Kingdom
UNSW	University of NSW
USL	United Services League
Vic.	Victoria
Vol.	Volume
WA	Western Australia
Wm	William

Watson Bibliography

In this bibliography only a few of the newspaper articles cited in the footnotes are included; similarly, entries in the excellent volumes of the ADB are retained in the footnotes rather than doubled-up here.

[ALP] *Third Commonwealth Political Labour Conference: Official Report, 1905*, The Worker, Brisbane, 1905.

[ALP] The Australian Labor Party, *Report of Proceedings of the Special Commonwealth Conference Called to Deal with Matters Arising out of the Conscription Issue*, Opened at Trades Hall, Melbourne, December 4th 1916 to December 9th 1916, J. Ashton for Labor Call, Melbourne, 1917.

Armstrong, Geoff and Rodney Cavalier, 'Trustees of the SCG and the Great War and the Flu Pandemic that Followed', *Southern Highlands Newsletter*, [publication of the Southern Highlands Branch of the ALP, NSW Branch], No. 238, May-June 2020, pp. 56- 67.

Ayres, Philip, *Prince of the Church. Patrick Francis Moran, 1830-1911*, The Miegunyah Press/Melbourne University Press, Carlton, 2007.

Beaumont, Joan, *Broken Nation: Australians in the Great War*, Allen & Unwin, Crow's Nest, 2013.

---- 'Similar, Yet Different: The Conscription Issue in Australia and New Zealand, 1916-17', *Journal of New Zealand Studies*, No. 27, 2018, pp. 2-15.

Barker, T.C., 'The International History of Motor Transport', *The Journal of Contemporary History*, Vol. 20, No. 1, 1985, pp. 3-19.

Bastian, Peter, *Andrew Fisher. An Underestimated Man*, UNSW Press, Sydney, 2009.

Bean, C.E.W. [and other authors], *The Official History of Australia in the War of 1914-1918*, in 12 volumes, Robert O'Neill, series editor, University of Queensland Press and the Australian War Memorial, St Lucia, 1981-1989 [edited and annotated from 1921-1936 originals].

Beattie, Belinda, 'Chris Watson's Resignation of the Federal Parliamentary Labor Party', *Media History*, Vol. 27, No. 3, 2021, pp. 285-298.

Belich, James, *The New Zealand Wars and the Victorian Interpretation of Racial Conflict*, Auckland University Press, Auckland, 1986.

— *Making Peoples. A History of the New Zealanders. From Polynesian Settlement to the End of the Nineteenth Century*, Allen Lane, the Penguin Press, Auckland, 1996.

— *Replenishing the Earth. The Settler Revolution and the Rise of the Anglo-World 1783-1939*, Oxford University Press, Oxford, 2009.

Bernstein, Eduard, *The Preconditions of Socialism*, Cambridge Texts in the History of Political Thought, Henry Tudor, editor and translator, Cambridge University Press, Cambridge, 1993.

Bolton, Geoffrey, 'How Uneasy Lies the Head? The Health of Australian Prime Ministers', *Health and History*, Vol. 1, No. 2/3, 1999, pp. 169-181.

Bongiorno, Frank *Dreamers and Schemers. A Political History of Australia*, La Trobe University Press in conjunction with Black Inc., Collingwood, 2022.

Catts, Dorothy, *James Howard Catts MHR*, Ure Smith Pty Ltd, Sydney, 1953.

— *King O'Malley: Man and Statesman. His Turbulent Life Story*, Publicity Press Pty Ltd, Sydney, 1957.

Clark, C.M.H., *A History of Australia. VI. 'The Old Dead Tree and the Young Tree Green' 1916-1935*, Melbourne University Press, Carlton, 1987.

Courtney, W.L. & J.E., *Pillars of Empire*, Jarrods Publishers, London, 1918.

Coward, Dan, The Impact of War on New South Wales, PhD thesis, ANU, Canberra, 1974.

Cowper, Norman, 'Sir Galahad, the Dauntless Imp, and Others (Personalities in the First Twenty-Five Years of Federal Politics.)', *The Australian Quarterly*, Vol. 23, No. 2, June 1951, pp. 35-56.

Crick, Bernard, *In Defence of Politics*, Continuum, London, Fifth Edition, 2005.

— 'Politics as a Form of Rule: Politics, Citizenship and Democracy', in Adrian Leftwich, editor, *What is Politics: The Activity and its Study*, John Wiley & Sons, 2015, pp. 67-85.

The Cyclopedia of New South Wales, McCarron, Stewart & Co, Sydney, 1907.

The Cyclopedia of New Zealand, Vol. 4, Otago and Southland Provincial Districts, Cyclopedia Company, Ltd., Christchurch, 1905.

Dalton, B.J., *War and Politics in New Zealand 1855-1870*, Sydney University Press, Sydney, 1967.

Day, David, *Andrew Fisher, Prime Minister of Australia*, Fourth Estate, London, 2008.

Deakin, Alfred, *Federated Australia. Selections from Letters to the Morning Post 1900-1910*, J.A. La Nauze, editor, Melbourne University Press, Carlton, 1968.

Dooley, Chris, *Redmond – A Life Undone. The Definitive Biography of John Redmond, the Forgotten Hero of Irish Politics*, Gill and Macmillan, 2015.

Dyrenfurth, Nick, *Heroes & Villains. The Rise and Fall of the Early Australian Labor Party*, Australian Scholarly Publications, North Melbourne, 2011.

Easson, Michael, editor, *McKell. The Achievements of Sir William McKell*, Allen & Unwin, Sydney, 1988.

— 'What it Means to be Labor', Michael Easson, editor, *The Foundation of Labor*, Lloyd Ross Forum and Pluto Press, Leichhardt, 1990, pp. 71-80.

— 'Burke and Australian Labor', Damien Freeman, editor, *The Market's Morals: Responding to Jesse Norman*, The Kapunda Press/Connor Court Publishing, Redland Bay [Queensland], 2020, pp. 57-77.

— '1954. The Third Great Labor Split', in *Tocsin, journal of the John Curtin Research Centre*, Issue 20, Special edition: Labor First in the World: Labor Making Australian History, March 2024, pp. 30-33.

Ellem, Bradon, *In Women's Hands? A History of Clothing Trades Unionism in Australia*, New South Wales University Press, Kensington, 1989.

Ellis, M.H., 'Watson – The Forgotten Man', *The Bulletin*, Vol. 84, No. 4305, 18 August 1962, pp. 28-31.

Evatt, Herbert Vere, *Australian Labour Leader. The Story of W.A. Holman and the Labour Movement*, Angus and Robertson, Sydney, 1940.

Faulkner, John & Stuart Macintyre, editors, *True Believers. The Story of the Federal Parliamentary Labor Party*, Allen & Unwin, Crows Nest, 2001.

Finkelstein, David, '"Jack's as Good as His Master": Scots and Print Culture in New Zealand, 1860-1900', *Book History*, Vol. 6, 2003, pp. 95-107.

Finnan, Joseph, *John Redmond and Irish Unity: 1912-1918*, Syracuse University Press, Syracuse [New York, USA], 2004.

Fitzgerald, John D., *The Rise of the Australian Labor Party*, Jubilee Fund of the Australian Labor Party, Worker Print, Sydney, 1915.

Ford, Patrick, *Cardinal Moran and the A.L.P.: A Study in the Encounter Between Moran and Socialism 1890-1907*, Melbourne University Press, Carlton, 1966.

Frappell, Ruth, 'John Watson. [Book Notes]', *Journal of the Royal Australian Historical Society*, Vol. 87, No. 2, December 2001, p. 300.

Freudenberg, Graham, *Cause for Power. The Official History of the New South Wales Branch of the Australian Labor Party*, Pluto Press, Leichhardt, 1991.

Gilchrist, Michael, *Daniel Mannix. Priest & Patriot*, Dove Communications, Blackburn [Victoria], 1982.

Graham, John McKay, The Voluntary System: Recruiting 1914-16, M.A. thesis in History, University of Auckland, 1971.

Graham, Morris, *A Toppled Labor Giant. Arthur Griffith: NSW's Revolutionary Minister for Public Works & Education*, self-published, Rutherford [NSW], 2017.

Grassby, Al and Silvia Ordonez, *The Man Time Forgot. The Life and Times of John Christian Watson, Australia's First Labor Prime Minister*, Pluto Press, Annandale, 1999.

The Griffith-Moroney Debate. Labor Party v. Socialist Labor Party, The People Printery, Sydney, Second Edition, 1909.

Hagan, Jim & Ken Turner, *A History of the Labor Party in New South Wales 1891-1991*, Longman Cheshire, Melbourne, 1991.

Haines, Robin F., *Emigration and the Labouring Poor: Australian Recruitment in Britain and Ireland, 1831-1860*, Macmillan, London, 1997.

Hamilton, Richard F. & Holger H. Herwig, *Decisions for War, 1914-1917*, Cambridge University Press, Cambridge, 2004.

Hawkins, John, 'Chris Watson: Australia's Second Treasurer', *Economic Round-up*, Commonwealth Treasury of Australia, Canberra, June 2007, pp. 119-127.

Hearn, Mark, 'Cultivating an Australian Sentiment: John Christian Watson's Narrative of White Nationalism', *National Identities*, Vol. 9, No. 4, pp. 351-368.

— 'Bound with the Empire: Narratives of Race, Nation, and Empire in the Australian Labor Party's Defence Policy, 1901-21', *War & Society*, Vol. 32, No. 2, 2013, pp. 95-115.

— '"The Benefits of Industrial Organisation"? The Second Fisher Government and *Fin de Siècle Modernity* in Australia', *Labour History*, No. 102, May 2012, pp. 37-54.

— '"Industrial Defence Against the Whole World": Deakinite New Protection as Narrative of Global Modernity', *Journal of Australian Studies*, Vol. 42, No. 3, 2018, pp. 343-356.

Hearn, Mark & Harry Knowles, *One Big Union. A History of the Australian Workers' Union 1886-1994*, Cambridge University Press, Cambridge, 1996.

— 'Struggling for Recognition: Reading the Individual in Labour History', *Labour History*, No. 87, 2004, pp. 1-10.

— 'Representative Lives? Biography and Labour History', *Labour History*, No. 100, May 2011, pp. 127-144.

Hogan, Michael, *Local Labor. A History of the Labor Party in Glebe, 1891-2003*, The Federation Press, Leichhardt, 2004.

— 'Template for a Labor Faction: The Industrial Section and the Industrial Vigilance Council of the NSW Labor Party, 1916-19', *Labour History*, No. 96, May 2009, pp. 79-100.

Hogan, Michael, editor, *Labor Pains, [Vol. I]: Early Conference and Executive Reports of the Labor Party of NSW [1891-1905]*, The Federation Press, Leichhardt, 2006.

— *Labor Pains, Vol. II: Early Conference and Executive Reports of the Labor Party of NSW, 1906-1911*, The Federation Press, Leichhardt, 2008.

— *Labor Pains, Vol. III: Early Conference and Executive Reports of the Labor Party of NSW, 1912-1917*, The Federation Press, Leichhardt, 2008.

Holloway, E.J., *The Australian Victory Over Conscription in 1916-17*, Anti-Conscription Jubilee Committee, Melbourne, 1966.

Holman, W.A., The Rise and Fall of the Federal Ministries - The Barton Ministry, *The Red Funnel*, Vol. 1, No. 3, October 1905, pp. 252-257.

— The Rise and Fall of the Federal Ministries - The Barton Ministry - Its Career, *The Red Funnel*, Vol. 1, No. 5, December 1905, pp. 371-376.

— The Rise and Fall of the Federal Ministries - The First Deakin Ministry, *The Red Funnel*, Vol. 1, No. 6, January 1906, pp. 508-512.

— The Rise and Fall of the Federal Ministries - The Watson Ministry, *The Red Funnel*, Vol. 2, No. 1, February 1906, pp. 45-51.

— The Rise and Fall of the Federal Ministries - The Reid Ministry, *The Red Funnel*, Vol. 2, No. 2, March 1906, pp. 160-165.

Hughes, Alan, 'Political Review', *The Australian Quarterly*, Vol. 41, No. 3, September 1969, pp. 87-98.

Hughes, Colin A., *Voting for the New South Wales Legislative Assembly, 1890-1964*, Research School of Social Sciences, ANU, Canberra, 1975.

Huntsman, Leone, 'Bounty Emigrants to Australia', *Clogher Record*, Vol. 17, No. 3, 2002, pp. 801-812.

Jauncey, Leslie C., *The Story of Conscription in Australia*, George Allen & Unwin, London, 1935.

Jordan, Deborah, 'Vance Palmer: Establishing Labor Daily Newspapers, 1910–1916', *Journal of Australian Studies*, Vol. 46, No. 2, 2022, pp. 147-163.

Jupp, James, 'Unitarians', James Jupp, editor, *The Encyclopaedia of Religion in Australia*, Cambridge University Press, Cambridge, 2009, pp. 581-582.

Kemp, David, *A Democratic Nation. Identity, Freedom and Equality in Australia 1901-1925*, The Miegunyah Press, Melbourne University Publishing Limited, Carlton, 2019.

Kimber, Julie & Peter Love, editors, *The Time of Their Lives. The Eight Hour Day and Working Life*, Melbourne Branch, Australian Society for the Study of Labour History, Melbourne, 2007.

Kirk, Neville [Review] Nick Dyrenfurth's *Heroes and Villains: The Rise and Fall of the Early Australian Labor Party*, Journal of Industrial Relations, Vol. 54, No. 1, 2012, pp. 96-98.

La Nauze, J.A., *Alfred Deakin. A Biography*, Vol. 1 & Vol. 2, Melbourne University Press, Carlton, 1965.

La Nauze J.A. and Elizabeth Nurser, editors, *Walter Murdoch and Alfred Deakin on Books and Men. Letters and Comments 1900-1918*, Melbourne University Press, Carlton, 1974.

Lansbury, Coral, 'William Guthrie Spence', *Labour History*, No. 13, November 1967, pp. 3-10.

Louis, L.J., *Trade Unions and the Depression. A Study of Victoria, 1930-32*, Australian National University Press, Canberra, 1968.

Louis, Wm. Roger, 'Australia and the German Colonies in the Pacific, 1914-1919', *Journal of Modern History*, Vol. 38, No. 4, December 1996, pp. 407-421.

Love, Peter, *Labour and the Money Power, Australian Labour Populism, 1890-1950*, Melbourne University Press, Carlton, 1984.

Macintyre, Stuart [Review] *The Man Time Forgot-The Life and Times of John Christian Watson, Australia's First Labor Prime Minister'*, *Times Literary Supplement*, 14 January 2000, p. 32.

Makin, Norman, *Federal Labour Leaders*, Union Printing, Sydney, 1961.

Malouf, David, *A Spirit of Play. The Making of Australian Consciousness*, [1998 Boyer Lectures broadcast on ABC radio], ABC Books, Sydney 1998.

Mannix, Patrick, *The Belligerent Prelate: An Alliance between Archbishop Daniel Mannix and Eamon de Valera*, Cambridge Scholars Publishing, Cambridge, 2012.

Markey, Raymond, *The Making of the Labor Party in New South Wales 1880-1900*, New South Wales University Press, Kensington, 1988.

— *In Case of Oppression. The Life and Times of the Labor Council of New South Wales*, Pluto Press with the Lloyd Ross Forum, Leichhardt, 1994.

McMullin, Ross, *The Light on the Hill. The Australian Labor Party, 1891-1991*, Oxford University Press Australia, Oxford, 1991.

— *So Monstrous a Travesty: Chris Watson and the World's First National Labor Government*, Scribe Publications, 2004.

McQueen, H., 'Who Were the Conscriptionists? Notes on Federal Labor Members', *Labour History*, No. 16, May 1969, pp. 44-48.

Meaney, Neville, *The Search for Security in the Pacific 1901-14, Vol. I of A History of Australian Defence and Foreign Policy, 1901-23*, Sydney University Press, Sydney, 1976.

Meaney, Neville, *Australia and the World Crisis, 1914-1923, Vol. II: A History of Australian Defence and Foreign Policy, 1901-23*, Sydney University Press, Sydney, 2009.

Moore, Tod, 'Liberal Imperialism in Australian Political Thought, 1902-14', *The Journal of Imperial and Commonwealth History*, Vol. 43, No. 1, 2015, pp. 58-79.

Nairn, Bede, 'J.C. Watson in New South Wales Politics, 1890-1894', *Journal of the Royal Australian Historical Society*, Vol. 48, Pt.2, June 1962, pp. 81-104.

— 'The 1916-17 Labor Party Crisis in New South Wales and the Advent of W. J. McKell', *Labour History*, No. 16, May 1969, pp. 3-13.

— *Civilising Capitalism. The Labor Movement in New South Wales 1870-1900*, Australian National University Press, Canberra, 1973.

— 'J.C. Watson, a Genealogical Note', *Labour History*, No. 34, May 1978, pp. 102-103.

— 'The NSW Labor Party, The Legislative Council and Catholics 1891-1926', Journal of the Royal Australian Historical Society, Vol. 71, Part 4, April 1986, pp. 235-254.

Niall, Brenda, *Mannix*, Text Publishing, Melbourne, 2015.

Palmer, Nettie, *Henry Bournes Higgins. A Memoir*, George G. Harrap & Company Ltd., London, 1931.

Perks, Murray Foreign and Defence Policies and Policy Making in the Australian Labor Parties, 1916-30, Master of Arts thesis, ANU, October 1974.

Rawson, D.W., The Organisation of the Australian Labor Party 1916-1941, PhD thesis, School of Political Science, Criminology and Sociology, Arts, The University of Melbourne, 1954.

Rawson, Don, 'McKell and Labor Unity', Michael Easson, editor, *McKell. The Achievements of Sir William McKell*, Allen & Unwin, Sydney, 1988, pp. 26-49.

Reeves, William Pember, *The Long White Cloud. Ao Tea Roa*, Horace Marshall & Don, London, 1898.

Reid, George H.S., *My Reminiscences*, Cassell and Company, London, 1917.

Robinson, Kenneth Wade, A History of the Political Labour Movement in New Zealand, 1850-1913, MA Thesis in History, Canterbury

University College, Christchurch, New Zealand, November 1937, 128pp.

Rogers, Thomas James, 'The Great Strikes of 1890-94: A Labour Historiography', *Melbourne Historical Journal*, Vol. 42, No. 1, 2014, pp. 85+.

Roydhouse, Thomas R. and H.J. Taperall, *The Labour Party in New South Wales. A History of its Formation and Legislative Career*, Edwards, Dunlop & Co., Limited, Sydney 1892.

Salmond, J.D., *New Zealand Labour's Pioneering Days. The History of the Labour Movement in NZ from 1840 to 1894*, edited by Desmond Crowley, Forward Press, Auckland, 1950.

Sammut, Jeremy, 'The Long Demise of the White Australia Policy', *Quadrant*, Vol. 49, No. 11, 2005, pp. 34–47.

Sanders, Noel, 'Private Faces in Public Spaces: The NRMA, 1920-51', in Helen Wilson, editor, *Australian Communications and the Public Sphere*, Palgrave, London, 1989, pp. 208-231.

Sawer, Geoffrey, *Australian Federal Politics and Law 1901-1929*, Melbourne University Press, Carlton, 1956.

Southerwood, W.T., *Catholics in British Colonies: Planting a Faith Where No Sun Sets. Islands and Dependencies of Britain to 1900*, Minerva Press, London & Sydney, 1998.

Spigelman, Jim, 'Institutional Feudalism and the NRMA', *The Australian Quarterly*, Vol. 43, No. 1, March 1971, pp. 20-28.

Stephenson, 'Scott, "Ballot-Faking Crooks and a Tyrannical Executive": The Australian Workers Union Faction and the 1923 New South Wales Labor Party Annual Conference', *Labour History*, No. 105, November 2013, pp. 93-111

Strangio, Paul and Nick Dyrenfurth, editors, *Confusion: The Making of the Australian Two-Party System*, Melbourne University Press, Carlton, 2009.

Tampke, Jurgen, editor, *Wunderbar Country. Germans Look at Australia, 1850-1914*, Hale & Iremonger, Sydney, 1982.

Thompson, Roger C., 'The Labor Party and Australian Imperialism in the Pacific, 1901-1919', *Labour History*, No. 23, November 1972, pp. 27-37.

Tsokhas, Kosmas, 'W.M. Hughes, The Commonwealth Line and the British Shipping Cartel, 1914-1927', *Prometheus, Critical Studies in Innovation*, Vol. 8, No. 2, 1990, pp. 288-303.

Turner, Henry Gyles, *The First Decade of the Australian Commonwealth. A Chronicle of Contemporary Politics 1901-1910*, Mason, Firth & McCutcheson, Melbourne, 1911.

Walker, R.B., *The Newspaper Press in New South Wales 1803-1920*, Sydney University Press, Camperdown, 1976.

J.C. Watson, 'A White or Piebald Australia', *United Australia*, Vol. 2, No. 6, 20 December 1901, pp. 7-9.

— 'Australian Defence', *The Call* [published by the Australian National Defence League, NSW Division], No. 1, August 1906, p. 6.

— 'Our Empty North. An Unguarded Gate', *The Lone Hand*, Vol. 1, No. 4, 1 August 1907, pp. 402-406.

— 'Our Empty North. The Prospects for the Future', *The Lone Hand*, Vol. 1, No. 6, 1 October 1907, pp. 678-682.

— 'Old-Age Pensions and Universal Service', *The Call* [published by the Australian National Defence League, NSW Division], No. 9, November 1908, pp. 10-11.

— [typed manuscript], The Labor Movement, n.d., circa 1914, NLA MS 451/2.

— 'Labor's First Eighteen. Men and Deeds from Our Magic Past', *The Sun* [Sydney, NSW], 8 May 1927, p. 27.

Weber, Max, 'Politics as a Vocation', in H.H. Gerth and C. Wright Mills, translators and editors, *From Max Weber: Essays in Sociology*, Routledge & Kegan Paul Ltd., London, 1946, pp. 77-128.

Weller, Patrick and Beverley Lloyd, editors, *Federal Executive Minutes 1915-1955*, Melbourne University Press, Carlton, 1978.

Weller, Patrick, editor, *Caucus Minutes 1901-1949: Vol. 1, 1901-1917*, Melbourne University Press, Carlton, 1975.

— *Caucus Minutes 1901-1949: Vol. 2, 1917-1931*, Melbourne University Press, Carlton, 1975.

— *Caucus Minutes 1901-1949: Vol. 3, 1932-1949*, Melbourne University Press, Carlton, 1975.

Withycombe, S.M., 'Trout Diplomacy: The Role of the Rainbow Trout in the Selection of Canberra as the Site for the Federal Capital City', *Canberra Historical Journal*, No. 61, 2008, pp. 10-16. https://search.informit.org/doi/10.3316/ielapa.200903931, accessed 3 November 2023.

Endnotes

Chapter 1: Watson and the Labor Story

[1] Bede Nairn, 'J.C. Watson in New South Wales Politics, 1890-1894', *Journal of the Royal Australian Historical Society*, Vol. 48, Pt.2, June 1962, p. 85.

[2] In and Out of Parliament. "Chris" Watson, *Freeman's Journal* [Sydney, NSW], 1 May 1919, p. 22.

[3] Rosemary Broomham, *On the Road: The NRMA's First Seventy-Five Years*, Allen & Unwin, St. Leonards, 1996, p. xvi.

[4] Patrick Weller, editor, *Caucus Minutes 1901-1949: Vol. 3, 1932-1949*, Melbourne University Press, Carlton, 1975, p. 296.

[5] 'The Hon. John Christian Watson, MHR', *The Cyclopedia of New South Wales*, McCarron, Stewart & Co, Sydney, 1907, p. 121.

[6] Al Grassby and Silvia Ordonez, *The Man Time Forgot. The Life and Times of John Christian Watson, Australia's First Labor Prime Minister*, Pluto Press, Annandale, 1999.

[7] Arthur Hoyle, 'O'Malley, King (1858-1953)', ADB, National Centre of Biography, ANU, https://adb.anu.edu.au/biography/omalley-king-7907/text13753, published first in hardcopy 1988, accessed online 13 January 2024.

[8] Dorothy Catts, *King O'Malley: Man and Statesman. His Turbulent Life Story*, Publicity Press Pty Ltd, Sydney, 1957, p. 75.

[9] Ibid. Presumably the embezzlement allegation was what won O'Malley forty shillings in damages.

[10] Dorothy Catts' biography reveals that O'Malley proudly spoke of his American origin and heritage later in life. He gave up the pretence. Dorothy Catts, *King O'Malley: Man and Statesman*, Loc. Cit., p. 261.

[11] Cf. Helen Irving, 'The Concept of Allegiance in Citizenship Law and Revocation: An Australian Study', *Citizenship Studies*, Vol. 23, Iss. 4, 2019, pp. 372-387; Matthew Stubbs & Adam Webster, 'Eligibility of Dual Citizens: The Coming-of-Age of Section 44', *Bulletin of the Law Society of South Australia*, Vol. 40, No. 1, February 2018, pp. 6; 8-9.

[12] Al Grassby and Silvia Ordonez, Loc. Cit., p. 7. Grassby and Ordonez say this child was supposedly to Watson, who owned the vessel, none of which could be true. See the next chapter.

[13] Ibid., p. 5.

[14] J.C. Watson [typed manuscript], The Labor Movement, n.d., circa 1914, NLA MS 451/2.

[15] Reference to and quotes from his paper appeared in the press. Cf. British Association, *The Argus* [Melbourne, Victoria], 25 July 1914, p. 18.

[16] Kim E. Beazley, Labor's Youngest PM, *Canberra Times*, 18 January 1966, p. 2.

[17] Stuart Macintyre, Note on Al Grassby & Silvia Ordonez, *The Man Time Forgot* (1999), *Times Literary Supplement*, 14 January 2000, p. 32.

[18] Geoffrey Sawer, *Australian Federal Politics and Law 1901-1929*, Melbourne University Press, Carlton, 1956, p. 327.

[19] Justice Higgins in the Harvester Decision decided that 7 shillings a day, or 42 shillings a week, was fair and reasonable wages for an unskilled labourer. This became the basis of Australia's national minimum wage system. Cf, in a vast literature, P.G. McCarthy, 'Justice Higgins and the Harvester Judgement', *Australian Economic History Review*, Vol. 9, Iss. 1, March 1969, pp. 17-38.

[20] Sawer, Loc. Cit., fn. 21, p. 37.

[21] Ibid., p. 327.

[22] Jottings. The Industrial World, *Otago Daily Times* [New Zealand], Issue 14174, 28 March 1908, p. 14.

[23] Ross McMullin, *So Monstrous a Travesty: Chris Watson and the World's First National Labor Government*, Scribe Publications, 2004, pp. 15-16.

[24] Rüdiger Dornbusch (1942-2002) sketched this idea in his Munich Lectures in Economics delivered on 17 November 1998, at the Center for Economic Studies of Ludwig-Maximilians-Universität. He died before completing a book on this theme. The 'law' is stated by Nobel-Prize winner Paul Krugman, Dornbusch's former student at MIT: Turmoil for Turkey's Trump, *The New York Times*, 24 May 2018.

[25] For a reference to Dornbusch's Law and Australian Labor, see: Michael Easson, '1954. The Third Great Labor Split', in *Tocsin, journal of the John Curtin Research Centre*, Issue 20, Special edition: Labor First in the World: Labor Making Australian History, March 2024, pp. 30-33.

[26] Max Weber, 'Politics as a Vocation', in H.H. Gerth and C. Wright Mills, translators and editors, *From Max Weber: Essays in Sociology*, Routledge & Kegan Paul Ltd., London, 1946, p. 115.

[27] Ibid.

[28] Bede Nairn dedicated his book *Civilising Capitalism. The Labor Movement in New South Wales 1870-1900*, Australian National University Press, Canberra, 1973 to the memory of John Christian Watson.

[29] Bede Nairn, *Civilising Capitalism*, Loc. Cit., p. 165.

[30] Ibid., p. 36.

Chapter 2: New Zealand Made

[1] Cf. "An Old Friend", Watson. As I Knew Him, *The Catholic Press* [Sydney, NSW], 26 May 1904, p. 15. The author of this article says he knew Watson from 1880/1881, had worked as an apprentice compositor with Watson, and settled in Sydney ahead of Watson, where they once shared lodgings in a boarding-house. The writer says of Watson: "His father was dead, and he lived with his mother and stepfather…", suggesting knowledge of at least some of the 'back story'.

[2] Section 44 (i) of the Australian Constitution disqualifies any person who owes a foreign allegiance, including citizenship of another country, from sitting as a member of Parliament.

[3] Tasmanian Names Index, recording arrivals in the colony, https://librariestas.ent.sirsidynix.net.au/client/en_AU/names/search/results?qf=NI_INDEX%09Record+type%09Arrivals%09Arrivals&qu=Minchin#, accessed 28 December 2023.

[4] It appears young William Minchin drowned at sea aged 18: "The brig Emma Prescott left Newcastle on the 29th ultimo, with a cargo of coal, bound to Melbourne. … on the following day a fresh breeze with a heavy rolling sea set in. The mainmast being sprung, Capt. Staunton found it necessary to reduce his canvas, and a sufficient compliment of hands was sent aloft to take in sail. One man, an ordinary seaman, named William Minchin, who was reefing the main topsail, fell overboard and was drowned. It is believed his parents are residents of Hobart Town…". Miscellaneous Shipping, *The Hobart Town Advertiser* [Tasmania], 23 June 1860, p. 2. I am grateful to Professor Catherine Watson for drawing this article to my attention.

[5] A good deal of the research underpinning the Watson story stands on the shoulders of Professor Catherine Watson's and her family's detective work. While finalising this chapter came surprises. For example, four birth certificates, sighted by Catherine Watson, of half-siblings of J.C. Watson, which show where the mother and father were born, adds to the confusion. Martha is listed as born in Liverpool, and George in Glasgow. Further, in Martha's *Hymnary* (on which, see a separate note) she wrote at the front, decipherable now only through a poor photocopy, that she was born in Liverpool. Did she mean 'came from Liverpool' – as in migrated from there? As for Watson Snr, his family was in Scotland. Perhaps they wanted descendants to look where remaining family were. Liverpool Minchins, the Scots Watsons. But who knows. There are so many maze detours and some false leads in the Watson mystery trail. Cf. Catherine Watson to Michael Easson [email], 8 February 2024.

[6] Descriptive List of Immigrants for July 1854, Tasmania, Australia, Passenger Arrivals, 1829-1957, accessed at https://libraries.tas.gov.au/Digital/CB7-12-1-3P17J2K on 14 January 2024.

[7] J. Matthew Gallman, *Receiving Erin's Children. Philadelphia, Liverpool, and the Irish Famine Migration, 1845-1855*, University of North Carolina Press, Chapel Hill, 2003, pp. 2-14; John Belchem, *Irish, Catholic and Scouse. The History of the Liverpool-Irish, 1800-1939*, Liverpool University Press, Liverpool, 2007, pp. 27-55; David Fitzpatrick, *Oceans of Consolation. Personal Accounts of Irish Migration to Australia*, Melbourne University Press, Carlton, 1995, pp. 6-19.

[8] Rules associated with the Bounty Migration Scheme are stated at: Bounty Immigration Regulations, *Colonial Times* [Hobart, Tasmania], 10 November 1853, p. 2. Cf. Robin F. Haines, *Emigration and the Labouring Poor: Australian Recruitment in Britain and Ireland, 1831-1860*, Macmillan, London, 1997; Leone Huntsman, 'Bounty Emigrants to Australia', *Clogher Record*, Vol. 17, No. 3, 2002, pp. 801-812.

[9] Bounty Regulations for the Promotion of Immigration, *Hobarton Guardian* [Hobart], 28 January 1854, p. 2.

[10] See: All Tasmania, Australia, Immigrant Applications and Bounty Tickets, 1854-1887 results for Minchin: https://www.ancestry.com/search/collections/2697/?name=_Minchin, accessed 31 December 2023, and details re Descriptive List of Immigrants for July 1854, Tasmania, Australia, Passenger Arrivals, 1829-1957, Loc. Cit.

[11] Cf. A.R. Love, 'Power, Robert (1794-1869)', ADB, National Centre of Biography, ANU, https://adb.anu.edu.au/biography/power-robert-2559/text3489, published first in hardcopy 1967, accessed online 31 December 2023.

[12] Victoria Coastal Passenger Lists, 1852-1924, Australia, https://www.familysearch.org/ark:/61903/1:1:DS8R-SG3Z, accessed 31 December 2023.

[13] Cf. 'William Minchin. Violent Theft; robbery. 27th October 1845', Old Bailey, London, records, https://www.oldbaileyonline.org/record/t18451027-2056?text=Minchin, accessed 31 December 2023.

[14] Catherine Watson to Michael Easson [email], 8 January 2024.

[15] Australian Convict Transportation Registers - Other Fleets & Ships, 1791-1868, https://www.ancestry.com.au/search/categories/40/?name=William_Minchin&location=5027&priority=australian, accessed on 31 December 2023.

[16] Libraries Tasmania - CON33-1-81 (stors.tas.gov.au), accessed 15 January 2024.

[17] In effect this meant for most 'ticket of leave' convicts, attendance at a Church of England or other Protestant services, as there were few Catholic Churches outside the main town, notwithstanding a third of the then population in Tasmania were Catholics. Cf. W.T. Southerwood, 'Van Diemen's Land', *Catholics in British Colonies: Planting a Faith Where No Sun Sets. Islands and Dependencies of Britain to 1900*, Minerva Press, London & Sydney, 1998, pp. 276-337.

[18] Tickets of Leave Granted, *The Britannia and Trades Advocate* [Hobart, Tasmania], 19 December 1850, p. 2.

[19] James Lord (1808-1881), https://oa.anu.edu.au/obituary/lord-james-22321, accessed 31 December 2023.

[20] Convict Department, *Launceston Examiner* [Tasmania], 20 September 1851, p. 12.

[21] Conditional Pardons Granted, *The Cornwall Chronicle* [Launceston, Tasmania], 15 January 1853, p. 4.

[22] I am grateful to Catherine Watson for urging me to entertain the point. We may never know. But the evidence might still be there, unearthed.

[23] New Zealand Death Certificate 1888001847, which states that Martha Watson had lived in New Zealand 25 years and her place of birth was Liverpool. Cf. Bede Nairn, 'J.C. Watson, a Genealogical Note', *Labour History*, No. 34, May 1978, p. 102. There is a discrepancy here, though. If Martha arrived in Tasmania, aged 7, and left for New Zealand in 1862, she would have been 15. No doubt, George Watson, her husband, would have filled out the details. He may not have known exactly. Accuracy in record keeping and recollection are not always perfect.

[24] New Zealand Marriage Certificate Registration Number 1866009460, marriage of "Martha Minchen and Johan Christian Tanck".

[25] Grassby and Ordonez say the actual ship name was the *La Joven Julia*: Al Grassby and Silvia Ordonez, Loc. cit., p. 13.

[26] Ibid. & Bede Nairn, 'J.C. Watson, a Genealogical Note', Loc. Cit., p. 102.

[27] Grassby and Ordonez, Loc. Cit., p. 12. The authors spell Tanck's middle name as Cristian rather than Christian.

[28] Married, *West Coast Times* [NZ], Issue 129, 15 February 1866, p. 2. Tarick must be a misspelling of Tanck. Not everyone's handwriting was copperplate.

[29] Catherine Watson to Michael Easson [email], 8 January 2024. This is Martha's hymnary.

[30] Catherine Watson to Michael Easson [email], 17 February 2024.

[31] Bede Nairn, 'J.C. Watson, a Genealogical Note', Loc. Cit., p. 102. Nairn's information must come from the newspaper report in the *West Coast Times*, as the record of the marriage certificate is silent as to witnesses.

[32] Grassby and Ordonez, Loc. Cit., p. 12.

[33] Ibid.

[34] Nairn, 'J.C. Watson, a Genealogical Note', Loc. Cit., p. 102.

[35] Copy of Wedding Certificate 13735/1925 obtained from the NSW Registry of Births Deaths & Marriage website, www.bdm.nsw.gov.au, accessed 1 July 2023.

[36] Catherine Watson to Michael Easson [email], 8 February 2024.

[37] Nairn, 'J.C. Watson, a Genealogical Note', Loc. Cit., p. 102.

[38] 1927-20 July 2014; notes of telephone conversation between Michael Easson and Jane Dunn, Jacqui's daughter, 30 December 2023.

[39] Quoted in Norman Abjorensen, 'Watson a British Subject', Loc. Cit.

[40] W.L. & J.E. Courtney, *Pillars of Empire*, Jarrod's Publishers, London, 1918, p. 213.

[41] The title of chapter 1 of their book.

[42] Grassby and Ordonez, Loc. Cit., p. 8.

[43] Ibid., p. 13.

[44] I cannot find details of this vessel in the Crew List Index Project (CLIP) which, admittedly, only concentrates on British merchant seafarers of the late 19th and early 20th century, rather than global records: Crew List Index Project. Nor can I find details for 1867 or 1868 of the wreck of any such ship named Julia or Joven Julia, WRECK WRAK EPAVE WRACK PECIO (wrecksite.eu)

[45] Grassby and Ordonez, Loc. Cit., p. 10.

[46] *Sue v. Hill (1999)*, HCA 30 (1999) CLR, 462.

[47] Cf. Norman Abjorensen, Johann, Not John, Likely Name of PM, *The Canberra Times*, 7 October 1993, p. 13; Norman Abjorensen, Watson a British Subject, *The Canberra Times*, 2 November 1993, p. 10.

[48] Later called the Waiareka school. [Anonymous], To the Editor, The Weston Jubilee, *The Otago Daily Times* [NZ], Iss. 20977, 17 March 1930, p. 5.

[49] Bede Nairn, 'Watson, John Christian (Chris) (1867-1941)', ADB, National Centre of Biography, ANU, https://adb.anu.edu.au/biography/watson-john-christian-chris-9003/text15849, published first in hardcopy 1990, accessed online 1 January 2024.

[50] People Talked About, *New Zealand Graphic*, Vol. 32, Iss. 20, 14 May 1904, p. 2. I am grateful to Professor Catherine Watson for drawing this profile to my attention.

[51] Grassby and Ordonez, Loc. Cit., pp. 16-17.

[52] Ibid., p. 17. Information on this point is attributed by the authors to David Marshall. But they must mean Russell Marshall, who is acknowledged at the beginning of their book, at p. ix.

[53] Notice, 'In Bankruptcy', posted by Julius & Balmer, Solicitors, *The North Otago Times* [NZ], Vol. 23, Iss. 1177, 20 January 1876, p. 3.

[54] Notice about a hearing on 2 February 1876 posted by Julius & Balmer, Solicitors, *The North Otago Times* [NZ], Vol. 23, Iss. 1183, 27 January 1876, p. 3. It appears the bankruptcy was discharged that February: Notice, *The North*

Otago Times [NZ], Vol. 23, Iss. 1193, 8 February 1876, p. 3

[55] Advertisement, *The Oamaru Mail* [NZ], Vol. 4, Iss. 830, 11 December 1878, p. 3.

[56] Advertisement for a Concert at the Cave Valley Schoolhouse in support of the Weston Cricket Club, *The Oamaru Mail* [NZ], Vol. 4, Iss. 1322, 3 October 1884, p. 3.

[57] Cf. *The Oamaru Mail* [NZ], Vol. 4, 10 November 1884, p. 2.

[58] Rifle Match, *Timaru Herald* [NZ], Iss. 3196, 23 December 1884, p. 3.

[59] See advertisements from 1884 to 1887. For example, Advertisement, *The Oamaru Mail* [NZ], Vol. 4, Issue 1322, 2 February 1884, p. 4; Ibid, Vol. 10, Iss. 3089, 6 November 1885, p. 4. Circulation leapt to 1500 in 1886 according to: Advertisement, *The Omaru Mail* [NZ], Vol. 10, Issue 3495, 15 April 1886, p. 1.

[60] For example, Advertisement, *The Omaru Mail* [NZ], Vol. X, Iss. 3905, 28 April 1887, p. 4; Advertisement, *The Oamaru Mail* [NZ], Vol. X, Iss. 4053, 24 October 1887, p. 1.

[61] 'Press', *The Cyclopedia of New Zealand, Vol. 4, Otago and Southland Provincial Districts*, Cyclopedia Company, Ltd., Christchurch, 1905, p. 525.

[62] Guy. H. Scholefield, *Newspapers in New Zealand*, A.H. & A.W. Reed, Wellington, 1958, p. 188.

[63] David Finkelstein, '"Jack's as Good as His Master": Scots and Print Culture in New Zealand, 1860-1900', *Book History*, Vol. 6, 2003, p. 105.

[64] J.A. La Nauze, *Alfred Deakin. A Biography*, Vol. 2, Melbourne University Press, Carlton, 1965, fn. at p. 240.

[65] FOR Sale, Cheap, *The Oamaru Mail* [NZ], Vol. 10, Iss. 3516, 12 May 1886, p. 3.

[66] The New Federal Premier, *Opunake Times* [NZ], Vol. 20, Iss. 638, 6 May 1904, p. 3.

[67] "An Old Friend", Watson. As I Knew Him, *The Catholic Press* [Sydney, NSW], 26 May 1904, p. 15.

[68] Ibid.

[69] Ibid.

[70] Tom Brooking, *The History of New Zealand*, Greenwood Press, Westport [Connecticut, USA], 2004, especially chapter 5, 'Boom and Bust, 1860-1890', pp. 67-76.

[71] Ex-Labour Leader, *Sun* [Auckland, NZ], Vol. 3, Iss. 848, 17 December 1929, p. 10.

[72] Personal, *Manawatu Standard* [NZ], Vol. 50, Iss. 41, 15 January 1930, p. 6.

[73] [No title], *The Illawarra Mercury* [Wollongong, NSW], 25 April 1930, p. 7.

See also: The Late James Mitchell, *The Otago Daily Times* [NZ], 11 January 1930, p. 19.

[74] Long Caree, *Evening Post* [NZ], Vol. 109, Iss. 6, 8 January 1930, p. 8.

[75] M.H. Ellis, "Watson – The Forgotten Man", *The Bulletin* [Sydney], Vol. 84, No. 4305, 18 August 1962, p. 28.

Chapter 3: Australian Made

[1] The phrase used in James Belich, *Replenishing the Earth. The Settler Revolution and the Rise of the Anglo-World 1783-1939*, Oxford University Press, Oxford, 2009, p. 261.

[2] For a recent, brief contextualising of the interaction, clashes, misunderstandings, and brutal subjugation of Aboriginal societies, see: Frank Bongiorno, *Dreamers and Schemers. A Political History of Australia*, La Trobe University Press in conjunction with Black Inc., Collingwood, 2022, pp. 7-23.

[3] Dan Coward, *Out of Sight: Sydney's Environmental History, 1851-1981*, ANU Press, Canberra, 1988, pp. 10; 52-53.

[4] James Belich, *Making Peoples. A History of the New Zealanders. From Polynesian Settlement to the End of the Nineteenth Century*, Allen Lane, the Penguin Press, Auckland, 1996, p. 317.

[5] Ibid.

[6] M.H. Ellis, 'Watson – The Forgotten Man', *The Bulletin*, Vol. 84, No. 4305, 18 August 1962, p. 28.

[7] English-born William Lane, journalist and socialist dreamer, active during the Great Shearers and Maritime Strikes in Australia, 1890-1891, convinced 500 hopeful Australians to board a ship and travel from Sydney to build a pure and perfect utopia in the wilds of Paraguay. See: Gavin Souter, 'Lane, William (1861-1917)', ADB, National Centre of Biography, ANU, https://adb.anu.edu.au/biography/lane-william-7024/text12217, published first in hardcopy 1983, accessed online 28 January 2024.

[8] Julie Kimber & Peter Love, editors, *The Time of Their Lives. The Eight Hour Day and Working Life*, Australian Society for the Study of Labour History, Melbourne, 2007, back cover summary. For explication, see the editors' 'Introduction', pp. 1-13.

[9] *Sydney Morning Herald*, 15 April 1891, p. 7.

[10] *Sydney Morning Herald*, 5 August 1892, p. 4.

[11] Michael Hogan, editor, *Labor Pains. Early conference and Executive Reports of the Labor Party of NSW*, The Federation Press, Annandale [NSW], 2006, pp. 50-52.

[12] L.F. Fitzhardinge, *William Morris Hughes. A Political Biography. Vol. 1: That Fiery Particle 1862-1914*, Angus and Robertson, Sydney, 1964, p. 42.

[13] Michael Hogan, editor, *Labor Pains. Early conference and Executive Reports of the Labor Party of NSW*, The Federation Press, Annandale [NSW], 2006, p. 101.

[14] Jim Hagan & Ken Turner, *A History of the Labor Party in New South Wales 1891-1991*, Longman Cheshire, Melbourne, 1991, p. 13.

[15] Minutes, 13 April 1893 & 2 May 1893, Trades and Labour Council of NSW, Executive Committee Minutes, SL of NSW MS A3824

[16] Minutes, 18 July 1893, Ibid.

[17] Young Labour Candidate, *Cootamundra Herald* [NSW], 27 January 1894, p. 5.

[18] Antony Green, '1894 Election Totals', *New South Wales Election Results 1856-2007*, Parliament of New South Wales, retrieved 23 November 2023.

[19] Watson: A Sketch. His Character ['All About People' column], *The Catholic Press* [Sydney, NSW], 10 March 1904, p. 14.

[20] Ibid.

[21] Representative Men. John Christian Watson MP, Federal Labor Leader, *Leader* [Melbourne, Victoria], 19 April 1902, p. 33.

[22] Watson: A Sketch. His Character ['All About People' column], Loc. Cit., p. 14.

[23] J.C. Watson [typed manuscript], The Labor Movement, n.d., circa 1914, NLA MS 451/2/1, p. 1.

[24] Martha Rutledge, 'O'Connor, Richard Edward (1851-1912), Senator for New South Wales, 1901-03 (Protectionist)', *The Biographical Dictionary of the Australian Senate*, vol. 1, 1901-1929, Melbourne University Press, Carlton South, Vic., 2000, pp. 27-30.

[25] Mark Hearn, 'Cultivating an Australian Sentiment: John Christian Watson's Narrative of White Nationalism', *National Identities*, Vol. 9, No. 4, 2007, pp. 351-368.

[26] In a considerable literature, see: C.N. Connolly, 'Miners' Rights: explaining the Lambing Flat riots of 1860-61', A. Curthoys & A. Markus, editors, *Who are our Enemies?: Racism and the Working Class in Australia*, Sydney, 1978; Karen Schamberger, Karen (31 July 2017). 'Difficult History in a Local Museum: The Lambing Flat Riots at Young, New South Wales', *Australian Historical Studies*, Vol. 48, No. 3, July 2017, pp. 436-441.

[27] J.C. Watson, "A White or Piebald Australia', *United Australia*, Vol. 2, No. 6, 20 December 1901, pp. 7-9.

[28] [Typed manuscript] J.C. Watson, [under sub-heading "White Australia"] The Labor Movement, n.d., circa 1914, NLA MS 451/2/1, p. 9.

[29] Ibid., p. 10.

[30] Ibid., p. 11.

[31] Federation Canvass, *Cootamundra Herald* [NSW], 20 February 1897, p. 5.

[32] Ibid.

[33] Roy Williams, *In God They Trust? The Religious Beliefs of Australia's Prime Ministers 1901-2013*, Bible Society Live Light, 2013, p. 26.

[34] On 27 November 1889 in the Unitarian Church, Liverpool Street, Sydney, Watson married English-born Ada Jane Low, a 30-year-old dressmaker.

[35] Williams, *In God They Trust?*, Loc. Cit., p. 48.

[36] A Pulpit Estimate of the Labor Premier, *The Daily Telegraph* [Sydney], 23 May 1904, p. 4.

[37] "Christian Socialism", *The Daily Telegraph*, 29 December 1904, p. 6.

Chapter 4: Labor's Leader

[1] Ibid. On the vote in caucus on 8 May 1901, see: Patrick Weller, editor, *Caucus Minutes 1901-1949: Vol. 1, 1901-1917*, Melbourne University Press, Carlton, 1975, p. 44.

[2] J.C. Watson, Labor's First Eighteen…, Loc. Cit.

[3] J.A. La Nauze, *Alfred Deakin. A Biography*, Vol. 2, Melbourne University Press, Carlton, 1965, p. 240.

[4] Ibid.

[5] Ibid.

[6] Representative Men. John Christian Watson MP, Federal Labor Leader, *Leader* [Melbourne, Victoria], 19 April 1902, p. 33.

[7] Geoffrey Sawer, *Australian Federal Politics and Law 1901-1929*, Loc. Cit., p. 37.

[8] "Ithuriel", Gallery Sketches. Among Federal Members, *The Australasian* [Melbourne, Victoria], 4 October 1902, p. 38. "Ithuriel" was the nom de plume of David H. Maling: Retirement of "Ithuriel", *The Australasian* [Melbourne, Victoria], 23 June 1923, p. 34.

[9] Research drawn from the University of Western Australia's database of Federal elections in Australia, Search for Australian election results, governments and parties in the Australian Politics and Elections Database (uwa.edu.au), accessed 1 October 2023, and cross-referenced with Colin A. Hughes and B.D. Graham, *A Handbook of Australian Government and Politics 1890-1964*, Australian National University Press, Canberra, 1968.

10 Views of Mr Watson, *Newcastle Morning Herald and Miners Advocate* [NSW], 26 January 1904, p. 4.

11 [typed manuscript] J.C. Watson, [under sub-heading 'Is Arbitration Successful?'] The Labor Movement, n.d., circa 1914, NLA MS 451/2/1, p. 7.

12 Ibid., p. 8.

13 Ibid.

14 Bernard Crick, *In Defence of Politics*, Continuum, London, Fifth Edition, 2005, p. 4. This classic was first published in 1962.

15 Bernard Crick, 'Politics as a Form of Rule: Politics, Citizenship and Democracy', in Adrian Leftwich, editor, *What is Politics: The Activity and its Study*, John Wiley & Sons, 2015, p. 69.

16 Representative Men. John Christian Watson MP, Federal Labor Leader, *Leader* [Melbourne, Victoria], 19 April 1902, p. 33.

17 Ibid.

18 Watson: A Sketch. His Character ['All About People' column], Loc. Cit., p. 14.

19 John Hawkins and Rob Van Den Hoorn, 'Poynton, Alexander (Alec) (1853-1935)', ADB, National Centre of Biography, ANU, https://adb.anu.edu.au/biography/poynton-alexander-alec-8093/text36763, published online 2021, accessed online 2 March 2024.

Chapter 5: Prime Minister Watson

1 [Cablegram] Lord Northcote [Henry Stafford Northcote] to The Right Honourable Secretary of State for the Colonies [The Rt. Hon. Alfred Lyttelton KC], 23 April 1904, NAA A6662, 237.

2 Photostat copy of secret despatch from the Governor General to the Secretary of State for the Colonies, 23 April 1904. NAA: CP201/1.

3 W.M. Hughes, *Policies and Potentates*, Angus & Robertson, Sydney, 1950, pp. 141-2.

4 W.A. Holman, 'The Rise and Fall of the Federal Ministries. The Watson Ministry', *The Red Funnel*, Vol. 2, No. 1, February 1906, p. 49.

5 Fourth Edition. News and Notes in a Nutshell, *The Herald* [Melbourne, Victoria]. 1 February 1904, p. 4.

6 The New Federal Ministry, *The Daily Telegraph* [Sydney, NSW], 27 April 1904, p. 7.

7 Dean Jaensch, 'Batchelor, Egerton Lee (1865-1911)', ADB, National Centre of Biography, ANU, https://adb.anu.edu.au/biography/batchelor-egerton-lee-82/text8641, published first in hardcopy 1979, accessed online 10 November 2023.

[8] J.C. Watson, Labor's First Eighteen. Men and Deeds from Our Magic Past, *The Sun* [Sydney, NSW], 8 May 1927, p. 27.

[9] Sir Frederick William Holder (1850-1909) was South Australian Premier for a second time, 1899-1901, with Batchelor in his ministry. He too was elected to the first Federal Parliament in 1901 and served as the country's first Speaker. See: Haydon Manning, 'Holder, Sir Frederick William (1850–1909)', *Australian Dictionary of Biography*, National Centre of Biography, Australian National University, https://adb.anu.edu.au/biography/holder-sir-frederick-william-6706/text36509, published online 2021, accessed online 10 November 2023.

[10] J.C. Watson, Labor's First Eighteen…, Loc. Cit.

[11] M.H.R. [Hugh Mahon], 'The Labour Forces in the Federal Parliament', *The Austral Light*, Supplement to Vol. 5, new series, No. 1, 1 June 1904, p. iv. McMullin identifies Mahon as the author of this article, *So Monstrous a Travesty*, Loc. Cit., fn. 68, p. 187.

[12] Sawer, *Australian Federal Politics and Law 1901-1929*, Loc. Cit., p. 40.

[13] [Typescript Letter] John Christian Watson to Lord Northcote, 13 August 1904. NAA: A 6661, 1079.

[14] [Typescript copy] Memo dated 15 August 1904, signed Northcote. NAA: A 6661, 1079.

[15] W.A. Holman, 'The Rise and Fall of the Federal Ministries. The Watson Ministry', Loc. Cit., p. 50.

[16] John Rickard, 'McLean, Allan (1840-1911)', ADB, National Centre of Biography, ANU, https://adb.anu.edu.au/biography/mclean-allan-7413/text12895, published first in hardcopy 1986, accessed online 7 March 2024.

[17] L.F. Fitzhardinge, *William Morris Hughes. A Political Biography. Vol. 1: That Fiery Particle 1862-1914*, Angus and Robertson, Sydney, 1964, p. 163.

[18] Graham Freudenberg, *Cause for Power. The Official History of the New South Wales Branch of the Australian Labor Party*, Pluto Press, Leichhardt, 1991, p. 75.

[19] To recall the title of McMullin's book on the Watson Government.

Chapter 6: Leaving the Parliament

[1] James Howard Catts, union secretary, politician, and businessman was the MHR for Cook, 1906-1922, who also from 1903-1913 was general secretary of the NSW Amalgamated Railway and Tramway Service Association See: Arthur Hoyle, 'Catts, James Howard (1877-1951)', ADB, National Centre of Biography, ANU, https://adb.anu.edu.au/biography/catts-james-howard-5535/text9429, published first in hardcopy 1979, accessed online 12 November 2023.

² John Grant, stonemason, union leader, political functionary, and politician, was the General Secretary of the Labor Party in NSW, 1903-1915. He was later a Labor Senator for NSW, 1914-20, & 1923-28. See: Geoffrey Hawker, 'Grant, John, 1857-1928', *The Biographical Dictionary of the Australian Senate*, Vol. 1, 1901-1929, Melbourne University Press, Carlton South, 2000, pp. 55-58.

³ J.C Watson to "Catts" [letter], 5 April 1906, p. 2. J.H. Catts Papers, NLA, MS 658/I/1 folder.

⁴ Ibid.

⁵ J.H. Catts to J.C. Watson [letter], 6 April 1906, p. 2. J.H. Catts Papers, NLA, MS 658/I/1 folder.

⁶ Letter, Watson to Deakin, 17 December 1906 marked Private and Confidential, Watson Papers, MS451/1/9, NLA.

⁷ On Heagney, carpenter, publican, and Labor radical: J. Bremner, 'Heagney, Patrick Reginald (1858-1922)', ADB, National Centre of Biography, ANU, https://adb.anu.edu.au/biography/heagney-patrick-reginald-7059/text11399, published first in hardcopy 1983, accessed online 9 November 2023. Patrick and Annie Agnes Heagney are now best known as the parents of labour movement activist and campaigner for women's equality, Muriel Heagney: J. Bremner, 'Heagney, Muriel Agnes (1885-1974)', ADB, National Centre of Biography, ANU, https://adb.anu.edu.au/biography/heagney-muriel-agnes-6620/text11399, published first in hardcopy 1983, accessed online 3 February 2024.

⁸ [ALP] *Official Report, Third Commonwealth Political Labour Conference 1905*, Worker Press, Brisbane, 1905 (held 8, 10-12 July 1905), p. 5.

⁹ Quoted in Patrick Ford, *Cardinal Moran and the ALP*, Loc. Cit., p. 268.

¹⁰ [ALP] *Official Report, Third Commonwealth Political Labour Conference 1905*, Loc. Cit., p. 10.

¹¹ Ibid.

¹² Ibid.

¹³ Ibid.

¹⁴ Ibid.

¹⁵ Ibid.

¹⁶ Ibid., p. 12.

¹⁷ Ibid.

¹⁸ Scottish-born Smeaton was an architect, unionist, and politician, who was educated at the Free Church Normal Seminary, Glasgow: B.K. Hyams, 'Smeaton, Thomas Hyland (1857-1927)', ADB, National Centre of Biography, ANU, https://adb.anu.edu.au/biography/smeaton-thomas-hyland-8461/text14877, published first in hardcopy 1988, accessed online 3 February 2024. In 1917,

over conscription, Smeaton left Labor for the Nationalists.

[19] [ALP] *Official Report, Third Commonwealth Political Labour Conference 1905*, Loc. Cit., p. 13.

[20] Ibid., p. 14.

[21] Philip Ayres, *Prince of the Church. Patrick Francis Moran, 1830-1911*, The Miegunyah Press/Melbourne University Press, Carlton, 2007, p. 247.

[22] Ibid., p. 19.

[23] Ibid., p. 20.

[24] Ibid., p. 21.

[25] Ibid., p. 21.

[26] Letter: J.C. Watson to Members of the Federal Labor Party, 27 July 1905, p. 1, NLA MS 451/1/94.

[27] Ibid.

[28] Ibid., MS 451/1/95.

[29] Ibid., MS 451/1/96.

[30] Ibid.

[31] Woody Allen, 'The Scrolls', *The New Republic*, 1 September 1974,

[32] The Capital Site, *The Age* [Queanbeyan, NSW], 5 January 1904, p. 3.

[33] Capital Site, *The Argus* [Melbourne], 9 October 1908, p. 5.

[34] S.M. Withycombe, 'Trout Diplomacy: The Role of the Rainbow Trout in the Selection of Canberra as the Site for the Federal Capital City', *Canberra Historical Journal*, No. 61, 2008, pp. 10-16. https://search.informit.org/doi/10.3316/ielapa.200903931, accessed 3 November 2023.

[35] Sawer, *Australian Federal Politics and Law 1901-1929*, Loc. Cit., p. 65.

[36] The Real Cause of Mr Watson's Retirement, *The Age* [Queanbeyan], 5 November 1907, p. 2.

[37] [Email] Jane Dunn [Watson's granddaughter] to Michael Easson, 29 April 2024.

[38] Tewksbury was a mining investor, prospector, developer, and businessman, a pioneer of gold dredging methods in Victoria, Australia, and elsewhere. An investor in and director of Ampol, he succeeded Watson as Chair of that company in 1941: Colin Simpson, *Show Me a Mountain: The Rise of an Australian Company, Ampol*, Angus and Robertson, Sydney, 1961, p. 65. For an overview of Tewksbury's career, see: Margaret Steven, 'Tewksbury, William Pearson (1869-1953)', ADB, National Centre of Biography, ANU, https://adb.anu.edu.au/biography/tewksbury-william-pearson-8774/text15381, published first in hardcopy 1990, accessed online 9 November 2023.

39 Political Points, *The Bulletin*, Vol. 30, No. 1546, 30 September 1909, p. 24.

40 Mr J. Chris Watson. Still Loyal to Labor, *The Burrangong Argus* [NSW], 9 February 1910, p. 2.

41 Glasgow-born Edward Riley (1859-1943), Watson's successor as MHR for Bland, held the seat for Labor from 1910 to 1931. Death of Former Federal Labor Member, *The Worker* [Brisbane, Qld], 2 August 1943, p. 9.

42 Federal Elections. Labour's Late Leader. Mr J.C. Watson's Swan Song. Unshaken Faith in the Labour Party, *Sydney Morning Herald*, 4 March 1910, p. 8.

43 The Fusion and the Caucus, *Sydney Morning Herald*, 23 March 1910, p. 6.

44 Labour Party, *Sydney Morning Herald*, 23 December 1915, p. 3. Technically, the ALP executive was then known as the Executive of the Political Labor League.

Chapter 7: Short Triumph of Laborism

1 Graham Freudenberg, *Cause for Power*, Loc. Cit., p. 7.

2 Minutes, 11 March 1890, Trades and Labour Council of NSW, Executive Committee Minutes, SL of NSW, MS A3823.

3 Minutes, 11 March, 8 April, 6 May 1890, Ibid.

4 See the collection of articles in Nick Dyrenfurth and Paul Strangio, editors, *Confusion. The Making of the Australian Two-Party System*, Melbourne University Press, Carlton, 2009.

5 West was MHR for East Sydney, 1910-1931. See: Frank Farrell, 'West, John Edward (1852-1931)', ADB, National Centre of Biography, ANU, https://adb.anu.edu.au/biography/west-john-edward-9051/text15949, published first in hardcopy 1990, accessed online 27 December 2023.

6 *Sydney Morning Herald*, 15 April 1891, p. 7.

7 M.H. Ellis, 'Watson – The Forgotten Man', *The Bulletin*, Vol. 84, No. 4305, 18 August 1962, p. 29. On Brady, see: John B. Webb, 'Brady, Edwin James (1869-1952)', ADB, National Centre of Biography, ANU, https://adb.anu.edu.au/biography/brady-edwin-james-5335/text9019, published first in hardcopy 1979, accessed online 6 December 2023.

8 Australian-born John "Jack" Daniel FitzGerald (1862-1922) printer, journalist, union official, barrister, and politician was elected for Labor as MLA for the multi-electorate of West Sydney in 1891, stood as a Protectionist MLA candidate in 1894, 1895 & 1898, lost as a Protectionist MHR candidate in 1901, and also lost as a MLA independent candidate in 1904. He rejoined the ALP in 1909, joined the central executive a few years later and was vice-president, 1912. Close to Holman, he was appointed MLC in 1915 and was expelled as a pro-conscriptionist in 1916. His ministries were Minister for Public In-

struction (1916), Health (1916-1919), Local Government (1916-1920), Justice and Solicitor General (1919-1920). He published: John D. Fitzgerald, *The Rise of the Australian Labor Party*, Jubilee Fund of the Australian Labor Party, Worker Print, Sydney, 1915. See: Bede Nairn, 'Fitzgerald, John Daniel (Jack) (1862-1922)', ADB, National Centre of Biography, ANU, https://adb.anu.edu.au/biography/fitzgerald-john-daniel-jack-6180/text10623, published first in hardcopy 1981, accessed online 2 December 2023.

[9] Andrew Joseph "Andy" Kelly (1854-1913) was MLA for West Sydney 1891-1894; he was expelled from the ALP for supporting the Dibbs Ministry in 1894; he was later re-admitted; he served as MLA for Sydney-Denison, 1901-1904, then for Lachlan, 1904 to his death, representing the ALP. See: Mr Kelly's Death. Pioneer Labour Member, *The Sydney Morning Herald*, 4 September 1913, p. 10.

[10] Bede Nairn, 'Davis, Thomas Martin (1856-1899)', ADB, National Centre of Biography, ANU, https://adb.anu.edu.au/biography/davis-thomas-martin-5916/text10077, published first in hardcopy 1981, accessed online 9 December 2023.

[11] Michael Easson, 'Burke and Australian Labor', Damien Freeman, editor, *The Market's Morals: Responding to Jesse Norman*, The Kapunda Press, Connor Court Publishing, Redland Bay [Queensland], 2020, pp. 58-59.

[12] Ibid., p. 69.

[13] Irish-born Arthur Hill Griffith (1861-1946), teacher, patent attorney, intellectual, and politician, served as a NSW MLA, 1894-1917, the first six years in the NSW Parliament with Watson. MP for Waratah, 1894-1903; Sturt, 1904-13; Annandale, 1913-1917. Secretary of the parliamentary party from 1894 until 1904. Member of NSW ALP central executive in 1896, 1903 until 1905, 1910; expelled from the ALP in 1916 over conscription, he still considered himself a Labor man. Resigned in opposition to Holman's coalition government in 1916 he stood as Independent Labor for Annandale in 1917, winning 49% of the vote but losing to the Labor candidate; sought readmission to the ALP thereafter; joined Federal Labor in 1931. Ministries included Public Works and most notably, from 1915-1916, Education. See: Morris Graham, *A Toppled Labor Giant. Arthur Griffith: NSW's Revolutionary Minister for Public Works & Education*, self-published, Rutherford [NSW], 2017, & Bede Nairn, 'Griffith, Arthur Hill (1861-1946)', ADB, National Centre of Biography, ANU, https://adb.anu.edu.au/biography/griffith-arthur-hill-6486/text11117, published first in hardcopy 1983, accessed online 18 November 2023.

[14] *The Griffith-Moroney Debate. Labor Party v. Socialist Labor Party*, The People Printery, Sydney, Second Edition, 1909, p. 5.

[15] James Molesworth, "One of the Pioneers". The Lame Tyrant of Paraguay –

Story of the Founding of' "New Australia", *Smith's Weekly* [Sydney NSW], 13 October 1923, p. 2

[16] Gavin Souter, *A Peculiar People. The Australians in Paraguay*, Sydney University Press, Sydney, 1968.

[17] Ethics of Labor Legislation, *The Age* [Melbourne, Victoria], 10 March 1902, p. 6.

[18] Billson, bootmaker, unionist, and politician: R. Kiss, 'Billson, John William (1862-1924)', ADB, National Centre of Biography, ANU, https://adb.anu.edu.au/biography/billson-john-william-5236/text8815, published first in hardcopy 1979, accessed online 30 December 2023.

[19] What Treachery is This?, *The Tocsin* [Melbourne, Victoria], 13 March 1902, p. 5.

[20] Unless explicitly stated otherwise, I quote from *The Age* story of Watson's speech.

[21] The quote is from Jeremy Bentham's chapter 17 of his *Introduction to the Principles of Morals and Legislation*. Cf. Jeremy Bentham, *A Fragment on Government with An Introduction to the Principles of Morals and Legislation*, Wilfred Harrison, editor, Basil Blackwell, Oxford, 1967, p. 411.

[22] Ethics of Labour Legislation. Speech by MHR Watson, *The Tocsin* [Melbourne, Victoria], 13 March 1902, p. 5.

[23] Quoted in Henry Tudor, 'Introduction', Eduard Bernstein, *The Preconditions of Socialism*, Cambridge Texts in the History of Political Thought, Henry Tudor, editor and translator, Cambridge University Press, Cambridge, 1993, p. xxviii. This book was published in German in 1899 and first translated into English in 1909 with the title *Evolutionary Socialism*; Watson, therefore, would not have been familiar with Bernstein's words.

[24] Ethics of Labour Legislation. Speech by MHR Watson, Loc. Cit.

[25] The author is not attributed here, but it is almost certainly L.F. Vernon's poem 'The Metamorphosis'. It is attributed to Vernon in its reproduction in *The Sacred Heart Review* [Cambridge and Boston, Massachusetts, USA], Vol. 37, No. 19, 4 May 1907, p. 312.

[26] Bede Nairn, *Civilising Capitalism. The Labor Movement in New South Wales 1870-1900*, Loc. Cit., pp. 186-187.

[27] Albert Métin, *Le socialisme sans doctrines: la question agraire et la question ouvrière en Australie et Nouvelle-Zélande (Socialism without Doctrines)*, F. Alcan, Paris, 1901, p. 281. Cf. Metin: *Socialism Without Doctrine*, translator, Russel Ward, Alternative Publishing Co-operative, Chippendale, 1977.

[28] For a representative samples of viewpoints, see: Jurgen Tampke, editor, *Wunderbar Country. Germans Look at Australia, 1850-1914*, Hale & Iremonger,

Sydney, 1982, especially Chapters 4, 5, and 8..

²⁹ The earliest reference to this phrase, that I have sourced, is 'Political Points' [column], *The Bulletin*, Vol. 11, No. 593, 27 June 1891, p. 10.

³⁰ Bede Nairn, 'Black, George Mure (1854-1936)', ADB, National Centre of Biography, ANU, https://adb.anu.edu.au/biography/black-george-mure-5250/text8845, published first in hardcopy 1979, accessed online 11 November 2023.

³¹ "Support in Return for Concessions", *The Australian Star* [NSW], 17 July 1891, p. 4.

³² Originally published in the late 1890s, Worker Trades Union Printery, Sydney; a second and third edition, subtitled 'A History from its Formation in 1891 Until 1904'; a fourth edition 'till Now' in 1906; the fifth edition in 1910, S.D. Townsend & Co., Sydney.

³³ T.J. Houghton & Co., Sydney, 1897; Workman Office, Sydney, Second Edition, n.d.; Australian Workman Print, Third Edition, n.d.; the earliest version covered the same ground as his *History*.

³⁴ Cf. The 1910 edition' chapter 1 began 'Evolution of Laborism – Objects and Platform of the New Party'.

³⁵ Fifth Edition, Loc. Cit., p. 32.

³⁶ John D. Fitzgerald, *The Rise of the Australian Labor Party*, Jubilee Fund of the Australian Labor Party, Worker Print, Sydney, 1915, p. 4.

³⁷ Nairn, *Civilising Capitalism*, Loc. Cit., p. 141.

³⁸ [ALP] *Third Commonwealth Political Labour Conference: Official Report, 1905*, The Worker, Brisbane, 1905, p. 13.

³⁹ Cf. Patrick Ford, *Cardinal Moran and the A.L.P.: A Study in the Encounter Between Moran and Socialism 1890-1907*, Melbourne University Press, Carlton, 1966, pp. 59-60.

⁴⁰ Eduard Bernstein, *The Preconditions of Socialism*, Loc. Cit., pp. 191-192.

Chapter 8: Unsettled Bargain on Defence

¹ Neville Meaney, *The Search for Security in the Pacific 1901-14*, Vol. I of *A History of Australian Defence and Foreign Policy, 1901-23*, Sydney University Press, Sydney, 1976, p. 51.

² "Ithuriel" [i.e., David H. Maling], Gallery Sketches. Among Federal Members, *The Australasian* [Melbourne, Victoria], 4 October 1902, p. 38.

³ J.C. Watson, 'Our Empty North. An Unguarded Gate', *The Lone Hand*, Vol. 1, No. 4, 1 August 1907, p. 402.

⁴ J.C. Watson [typed manuscript], [under sub-heading 'Attitude on Defence'] The Labor Movement, n.d., circa 1914, NLA MS 451/2/1, p. 13.

[5] Ibid.

[6] J.C Watson, 'Australian Defence', *The Call* [published by the Australian National Defence League, NSW Division], No. 1, August 1906, p. 6.

[7] Ibid.

[8] 'Political Notes', *The Call* [published by the Australian National Defence League, NSW Division], No. 1, August 1906, p. 17.

[9] 'Our Objects', *The Call* [published by the Australian National Defence League, NSW Division], No. 2, November 1906, p. 2.

[10] 'Mr J.C. Watson, MHR' [in the report on the League AGM], *The Call* [published by the Australian National Defence League, NSW Division], No. 6, November 1907, p. 21.

[11] J.C. Watson, 'Old-Age Pensions and Universal Service', *The Call* [published by the Australian National Defence League, NSW Division], No. 9, November 1908, p. 11.

[12] Ibid., p. 10.

[13] Ibid., p. 11.

[14] 'Labour Conference and Compulsory Military Training', *The Call* [published by the Australian National Defence League, NSW Division], No. 9, November 1908, p. 20.

[15] Ibid., p. 21.

[16] Ibid.

[17] Ibid., p. 22.

[18] Ibid.

[19] Ibid., p. 21. Oddly, Watson illustrated his claim of lack of preparation through an historical example, saying that Pizarro conquered the Incas in 1532 with a small force because the latter were poorly prepared and complacent. Actually, the Incas were warring with each other at the time the Spanish snaffled that territory.

[20] Labour Conference and Compulsory Military Training', *The Call*, Loc. Cit., p. 22.

[21] Neville Meaney, *Australia and the World Crisis, 1914-1923, Vol. II: A History of Australian Defence and Foreign Policy, 1901-23*, Sydney University Press, Sydney, 2009, p. 97. Cf Report in The Sydney Morning Herald, 13 May 1915.

[22] J.C. Watson [typescript] Labor Politics of Empire, Letter to the editor, *The Daily Citizen* [London, UK], 24 April 1915, NLA MS 451/1/125.

[23] Labour Politics of Empire…, *Daily Citizen*, 20 April 1915, Loc. Cit., p. 3.

[24] J.C. Watson [typescript] Labor Politics of Empire, Letter to the editor, Loc. Cit., MS 451/1/125-126.

25 Murray Perks, Foreign and Defence Policies and Policy Making in the Australian Labor Parties, 1916-30, Master of Arts thesis, ANU, October 1974, p. 3.

Chapter 9: Conscription, Expulsion and Aftermath

[1] Cf. Richard F. Hamilton & Holger H. Herwig, *Decisions for War, 1914-1917*, Cambridge University Press, Cambridge, 2004.

[2] "To The Last Man", *The Daily Telegraph*, 1 August 1914, p. 13.

[3] On July 28 Austria declared war on Serbia, on 2 August German troops entered France and Luxembourg and on 4 August Germany invaded and declared war on Belgium. Great Britain declared war on Germany.

[4] Cf. 'Chapter 1: Australia's Position at the Outbreak', C.E.W. Bean, *The Official History of Australia in the War of 1914-1918, Vol. 1: The Story of ANZAC*, Robert O'Neill, series editor, University of Queensland Press and the Australian War Memorial, St Lucia, 1981 [from the 1921 publication], pp. 1-19.

[5] Federal Politics. The Labour Manifesto. Prime Minister's Remarks, *The West Australian* [Perth], 27 August 1914, p. 8.

[6] Kosmas Tsokhas, 'W.M. Hughes, The Commonwealth Line and the British Shipping Cartel, 1914-1927', *Prometheus, Critical Studies in Innovation*, Vol. 8, No. 2, 1990, pp. 288-303.

[7] Joan Beaumont, 'Similar, Yet Different: The Conscription Issue in Australia and New Zealand, 1916-17', *Journal of New Zealand Studies*, No. 27, 2018, pp. 2-15; John McKay Graham, The Voluntary System: Recruiting 1914-16, MA thesis in History, University of Auckland, 1971.

[8] Universal Service League. List of Officers, *Universal Service* [publication of the NSW Branch, Universal Services League], No. 3, 12 August 1916, p. 7.

[9] Australian born Richard "Dick" Meagher, solicitor, land speculator, and politician, won the seat of Sydney-Phillip on in July 1895, as a Protectionist, but resigned over a legal controversy a little over two months later. As an independent, he won the Tweed in 1898 and 1901. His seat was abolished in 1904. Under various political colours, he served as an Alderman on the Council of the city of Sydney, 1901 to 1920. In 1907, as an independent, he defeated the Labor member for Phillip and once more was a MLA. Meagher joined the ALP in 1909, served on the NSW executive from 1910-16, vice-president in 1913 and 1915-16, and president in 1914-15. In the NSW parliament, he became Speaker in 1913, and in early 1916 he was appointed by the Holman government as the first Labor Lord Mayor of Sydney. Expelled from Labor over conscription in November 1916, as independent Labor he lost Phillip at the 1917 state elections to Jack Doyle, the NSW Labor party president. Holman appointed Meagher to the Legislative Council in 1917. He resigned to contest as an independent the multi-member state seat of Sydney on 20 March

1920, narrowly losing. See: Bede Nairn, 'Meagher, Richard Denis (Dick) (1866-1931)', ADB, National Centre of Biography, ANU, https://adb.anu.edu.au/biography/meagher-richard-denis-dick-7546/text13165, published first in hardcopy 1986, accessed online 30 November 2023; Mr R.D. Meagher, *Sydney Morning Herald*, 18 September 1931, p. 10.

[10] Ernest Scott, *The Official History of Australia in the War of 1914-1918, Vol. 11: Australia During the War*, Robert O'Neill, series editor, University of Queensland Press and the Australian War Memorial, St Lucia, 1989 [from the 1936 publication], p. 334.

[11] The Need for Immediate Action, *Universal Service* [publication of the NSW Branch, Universal Services League], No. 1, 15 July 1916, p. 1.

[12] Neville Meaney, *Australia and the World Crisis, 1914-1923, Vol. II: A History of Australian Defence and Foreign Policy, 1901-23*, Sydney University Press, Sydney, 2009, p. 50.

[13] The geologist and scientist Professor Edgeworth David was then president of the Universal Service League and a leading figure at recruiting rallies. See: D. F. Branagan and T. G. Vallance, 'David, Sir Tannatt William Edgeworth (1858-1934)', ADB, National Centre of Biography, ANU, https://adb.anu.edu.au/biography/david-sir-tannatt-william-edgeworth-5894/text10033, published first in hardcopy 1981, accessed online 10 December 2023.

[14] Conscription, *The Daily Telegraph* [Sydney, NSW], 17 September 1915, p. 8.

[15] Labor and Conscription. Opposition of Industrial Organisations. PLL Executive and Universal Service League, *The Australian Worker* [Sydney, NSW] 9 December 1915, p. 5. This resolution is referenced in Leslie C. Jauncey, *The Story of Conscription in Australia*, George Allen & Unwin, London, 1935, p. 12o.

[16] Lewis (1876-1935) was the secretary of the Flour Millers and Mill Employees' Union and the Storemen and Packers' Union. Expelled from the Labor party over conscription in 1916, he later became an industrial officer with the NSW Chamber of Manufactures and other employer bodies. Mr G. Lewis, *Sydney Morning Herald*, 2 November 1935, p. 12.

[17] Thompson, journalist, editor, and union official, was the General Secretary of the Amalgamated Railway Service Association, 1913-1920, and was jailed during the 1917 rail strike in NSW. In September 1916 at a public meeting before the first conscription referendum, he said his views had changed. On conscription: "He said that he had always been opposed to it, although at one time there appeared to be a possibility of the burden of war being equally distributed. That day, however, had passed." Railway Men. Against Conscription. Mr Claude Thompson's Denunciation, *National Advocate* [Bathurst, NSW], 19 September 1916, p. 5. See also: Labor Veteran Passes, *The Australian Work-*

er [Sydney, NSW], 7 September 1949, p. 5, & 'Thompson, Claude William (1876-1949)', Obituaries Australia, National Centre of Biography, ANU, https://labouraustralia.anu.edu.au/biography/thompson-claude-william-32918/text41005, accessed 4 December 2023.

[18] New Zealand-born Rae, shearer, AWU life member, was elected an MLA for Murrumbidgee in 1891, part of the first batch of Labor MPs in the NSW parliament; but lost the seat thereafter and failed in subsequent attempts to win lower house seats in the NSW and Federal parliaments. He won for Labor election to the Senate in 1910, lost in 1914, fell out with the leadership of the AWU after the War, and was re-elected a Labor Senator for NSW, 1928-1935, joining the breakaway Lang State Labor group in 1931: Frank Farrell, 'Rae, Arthur Edward (1860-1943)', ADB, National Centre of Biography, ANU, https://adb.anu.edu.au/biography/rae-arthur-edward-8148/text14237, published first in hardcopy 1988, accessed online 28 November 2023.

[19] Conscription. Opposed by PLL. A Spirited Debate, *Sydney Morning Herald*, 9 May 1916, p. 9.

[20] Perks, Loc. Cit., p. 178.

[21] Labor's Responsibility in World Crisis. Plain Words by Mr Hughes, *Universal Service* [publication of the NSW Branch, Universal Services League], No. 4, 26 August 1916, p. 5.

[22] The Referendum, *The Sydney Morning Herald*, 19 September 1916, p. 8.

[23] Coral Lansbury, 'William Guthrie Spence', *Labour History*, No. 13, November 1967, p. 10.

[24] Remarkable Scenes, *Sydney Morning Herald*, 19 September 1916, p. 9.

[25] Mr Watson's Support. Vigilance the Price of Liberty, *Sydney Morning Herald*, 19 September 1916, p. 10.

[26] Cf. Bede Nairn, 'The 1916-17 Labor Party Crisis in New South Wales and the Advent of W. J. McKell', *Labour History*, No. 16, May 1969, pp. 3-13.

[27] Conscription. Mr Hughes' Meeting. "Workers Solid", *National Advocate* [Bathurst, NSW], 21 September 1916, p. 4. Cf. Federated Boilermakers Condemn It. An Overwhelming Majority, *Australian Worker* [Sydney, NSW], 21 September 1916, p. 17.

[28] John William "Jack" Doyle (1875-1951) was President of the NSW PLL, 1916-1917, and NSW state MP for Phillip, 1917-1920, and MP for Balmain, 1920-1922. He was a leader of the No Conscription Campaign. Doyle gave up his seat of Balmain for Dr H.V. Evatt in 1922. See: 'Mr John William Doyle (1875-1951), former members of the Parliament of New South Wales, retrieved 8 November 2023.

[29] Conscription. Mr Hughes' Meeting. "Workers Solid", *National Advocate* [Ba-

thurst, NSW], 21 September 1916, p. 4

[30] J.C. Watson [letter to the editor] "Scabbing" on the Allies, *The Daily Telegraph* [Sydney, NSW], 3 October 1916, p. 6.

[31] Australia's Honour, *Sydney Morning Herald*, 25 October 1916, p. 7.

[32] Still Strong Labor Men, *Sydney Morning Herald*, 21 September 1916, p. 10.

[33] Compulsory Service and the Referendum. Mr Watson's Views, *The Scone Advocate* [NSW], 6 October 1916, p. 6.

[34] Morris Graham, *A Toppled Labor Giant. Arthur Griffith: NSW's Revolutionary Minister for Public Works & Education*, self-published, Rutherford [NSW], 2017, p. 202.

[35] Australian born James Guy Dalley Arkins, flour miller, builder, clerk, and country journalist, had a long political career after expulsion from the ALP. In February 1915 in a by-election, he won for Labor the state seat of Castlereagh. In March 1916 he enlisted in the AIF. For the Nationalists he held the seat in 1917 (a gentleman's agreement between the parties meant that seats held by combatant MPs were not contested). He continued as a NSW MLA to 1930, and again from 1938 to 1941. In between time, he was a UAP Senator, filling a casual vacancy, 1935-1937: David Clune, 'Arkins, James Guy Dalley (1887-1980), Senator for New South Wales, 1935-37, United Australia Party', *Biographical Dictionary of the Australian Senate, Volume 2, 1929-1962*, Melbourne University Press, Carlton, 2004, pp. 426-429.

[36] New Zealand born William Roy Clifford Bagnall (1882-1950), process engraver, union official, and politician, was NSW Labor MLA for St George, 1913-1916, then for the Nationalists to 1925, and again 1925-1927. See: former members of the Parliament of New South Wales, retrieved 28 November 2023.

[37] Australian born George Arthur Burgess (1863-1941), shearer and union official, succeeded Watson as a Labor MLA for Young in 1901; then after that seat was abolished, he held Burrangong to 1917. After expulsion from the ALP, he was defeated by Labor in his old seat as a Nationalist in state elections in 1917. See: former members of the Parliament of New South Wales, retrieved 28 November 2023.

[38] Australian born Thomas Crawford, Presbyterian minister, and politician was Labor MLA for Marrickville from 1910 to his expulsion and was defeated as a Nationalist candidate by Labor in the state election in 1917: L.G. Tanner, 'Crawford, Thomas Simpson (1875-1976)', ADB, National Centre of Biography, ANU, https://adb.anu.edu.au/biography/crawford-thomas-simpson-5812/text9865, published first in hardcopy 1981, accessed online 28 November 2023.

[39] English-born Alfred Edden (1850-1930), coal miner, trade union organiser, and politician, won election for Labor as MLA for Northumberland in the

famous 'Labor class of 1891', but refused to sign the 'pledge', then in 1894 successfully ran for Kahibah as independent Labor, rejoined Labor in 1895, and held the seat until 1920, his last term as a Nationalist. See: W.G. McMinn, 'Edden, Alfred (1850-1930)', ADB, National Centre of Biography, ANU, https://adb.anu.edu.au/biography/edden-alfred-6083/text10419, published first in hardcopy 1981, accessed online 28 November 2023.

[40] Arthur Rowland Gardiner (1876-1948), schoolteacher, builder, and politician, won Newcastle as a Labor MLA in 1910 and held the seat to 2022, the last six years as independent Labor. See: former members of the Parliament of New South Wales, retrieved 28 November 2023.

[41] English born Robert Hollis (1851-1937), engine driver, union official, and politician, from 1901 was Labor MLA for Newtown-Erskine, then Newtown to 1917, losing as a Nationalist candidate to Labor after his expulsion from the ALP. See: former members of the Parliament of New South Wales, retrieved 28 November 2023.

[42] Scottish born James Ballantine Mercer (1842-1925), insurance agent and politician, was Labor MLA for Rozelle 1910-1916, then after his expulsion from the ALP lost to Labor in 1917 when he stood as a Nationalist candidate. See: former members of the Parliament of New South Wales, retrieved 28 November 2023.

[43] Australian born James John Morrish (1868-1956), barman, union official, politician, and farmer, was Labor MLA for Rozelle 1910-1916, then after his expulsion from the ALP lost in 1917 as a Nationalist candidate. See: former members of the Parliament of New South Wales, retrieved 28 November 2023.

[44] English born John Barnes Nicholson (1840-1919), coal miner, union official and politician, was present at the parliamentary triumph of Labor in 1891. Elected that year MLA for Illawarra, he refused the 'pledge', stood as independent Labor in 1894, independent in 1895, Free Trade in 1898, independent Labor in 1901, then Labor – winning all those elections to 1904 as MLA for Woronora. As Labor he won Wollongong in 1904 and continued as a Labor MLA for the seat until expelled in 1916 over conscription; he lost to Labor in 1917 when he ran as a Nationalist candidate. See: former members of the Parliament of New South Wales, retrieved 28 November 2023.

[45] Scottish born Robert Scobie (1848-1917), saddler, storekeeper, and politician, stood unsuccessfully for Labor in NSW state elections for the country electorate of Wentworth in 1894, 1895, and 1898, before winning as the Labor MLA for the seat in 1904; after a redistribution, he stood successfully for Murray for Labor from 1907 onwards, and after ALP expulsion, winning again in 1917 as a Nationalist. He died suddenly five months later. See: Death of Mr Robert Scobie MLA, *Riverina Recorder* [NSW], 22 August 1917, p. 2.

⁴⁶ PLL. Mr J.C. Watson Expelled, *Sydney Morning Herald*, 4 November 1916, p. 12.

⁴⁷ Letter: P.C. Evans, General Secretary, Political Labor League Executive of NSW, to J.C. Watson, 4 November 1916, J.C. Watson Papers, NLA MS 451.

⁴⁸ On 14 November 1916, Black was expelled: Bede Nairn, 'The 1916-17 Labor Party Crisis in New South Wales and the Advent of W. J. McKell', *Labour History*, No. 16, May 1969, fn. 13 at p. 8.

⁴⁹ In a report in the Sydney press, Black is referred to as one of two independent Nationalist candidates. The Nationalists could not agree on a preferred candidate between Black and an officer of the Farmers' and Settlers' Association. See: The Elections, *The Daily Telegraph*, 5 March 1917, p. 4; Poor George Black, *North Western Courier* [NSW], 14 March 1917, p. 2.

⁵⁰ Mr. George Black, *North Western Courier* [NSW], 19 March 1917, p. 2. (A note published with this article said the text was "supplied by Mr Black's Organiser".)

⁵¹ Michael Hogan, 'Template for a Labor Faction: The Industrial Section and the Industrial Vigilance Council of the NSW Labor Party, 1916-19', *Labour History*, No. 96, May 2009, pp. 79-100.

⁵² New Zealand-born Lawrence Joseph O'Hara (1889-1919), public servant, was elected in 1919 as Labor MLA for Paddington, but died before being sworn-in, probably due to the Spanish 'flu. See: former members of the Parliament of New South Wales, retrieved 28 November 2023.

⁵³ Letter: J.C. Watson to L.J. O'Hara, Hon. Secretary, Paddington PLL, 13 November 1916, J.C. Watson Papers, NLA MS 451/1/91.

⁵⁴ Kim E. Beazley, Labor's Youngest PM [John Christian Watson], *The Canberra Times*, 18 January 1966, p. 2.

⁵⁵ The Elections. Campaign Addresses. Mr J.C. Watson. Speech at Prahran. Tyranny Denounced, *The Argus* [Melbourne, Victoria], 11 April 1917, p. 9.

⁵⁶ Maribyrnong. Mr J.C. Watson at Footscray. "Climbing Over the Tailboard of Labor", *The Age* [Melbourne, Victoria], 17 April 1917, p. 8.

⁵⁷ C.M.H. Clark, *A History of Australia. VI. 'The Old Dead Tree and the Young Tree Green' 1916-1935*, Melbourne University Press, Carlton, 1987, p. 47.

⁵⁸ Ibid.

⁵⁹ Maribyrnong. Mr J.C. Watson at Footscray. "Climbing Over the Tailboard of Labor", *The Age* [Melbourne, Victoria], 17 April 1917, p. 8.

⁶⁰ David Kemp, *A Democratic Nation. Identity, Freedom and Equality in Australia 1901-1925*, The Miegunyah Press, Melbourne University Publishing Limited, Carlton, 2019, p. 338.

⁶¹ New Party. May Embrace Existing Organisations. Mr Watson's Statement,

Sydney Morning Herald, 12 January 1917, p. 6.

[62] National Federation. Vigorous Organising Work, *Sydney Morning Herald*, 22 February 1917, p. 7.

Chapter 10: Why the Split Went So Deep …

[1] Vere Gordon Childe, *How Labour Governs, A Study in Workers' Representation in Australia*, The Labour Publishing Company Limited, London, 1923.

[2] This phrase was used by Gough Whitlam about a certain kind of calculating Labor figure who was seemingly perpetually personally torn as to whom to be most disloyal to. Alan Hughes, 'Political Review', *The Australian Quarterly*, Vol. 41, No. 3, September 1969, p. 93.

[3] Jim Hagan & Ken Turner, *A History of the Labor Party in New South Wales 1891-1991*, Longman Cheshire, Melbourne, 1991, p. 114.

[4] Wither? Organised Labor's Drift. Heading for Disaster. Mr J.C. Watson's Warning, *The Daily Telegraph* [Sydney], 12 October 1921, p. 6.

[5] Maribyrnong. Mr J.C. Watson at Footscray. "Climbing Over the Tailboard of Labor", *The Age* [Melbourne, Victoria], 17 April 1917, p. 8.

[6] Janet McCalman, 'Tudor, Francis Gwynne (Frank) (1866-1922)', ADB, National Centre of Biography, ANU, https://adb.anu.edu.au/biography/tudor-francis-gwynne-frank-8874/text15583, published first in hardcopy 1990, accessed online 12 March 2024.

[7] Herbert Vere Evatt, *Australian Labour Leader. The Story of W.A. Holman and the Labour Movement*, Angus and Robertson, Sydney, 1940, pp. 386ff.

[8] Evans was accused of "disloyalty". Asked if he had been given a chance to defend himself, the new ALP General Secretary, William Carey explained: "Mr. Evans had not, but he had automatically placed himself out of the movement by fraternising with the Nationalist leaders." See: Mr. P.C. Evans Expelled, *Goulburn Evening Penny Post*, 20 January 1920, p. 4. Evans had hoped to run for Labor as the candidate for Goulburn but ended up running as a Labor independent at the state elections on 20 March 1920, which Bailey won. Evans sued Bailey for defamation and, ultimately in 1925 Evans won £50 damages. Bailey had alleged Evans was financed by the Nationalist Party in the 1920 election for Goulburn. Cf.: £1000 Defamation Action, *Leader* [Orange, NSW], 19 June 1925, p. 6. Evans died in Hong Kong: Deaths, *Sydney Morning Herald*, 24 March 1934, p. 14. A profile on Evans' PLL General-Secretary successor, Carey: The Party Bosses, *Evening News* [Sydney, NSW], 13 December 1922, p. 8.

[9] Mr. P.C. Evans' Candidature, *The Yass Courier* [NSW], 19 February 1920, p. 2.

[10] Cf. Don Rawson, 'McKell and Labor Unity', Michael Easson, editor, *McKell. The Achievements of Sir William McKell*, Allen & Unwin, Sydney, 1988, pp. 26-49.

[11] Peter Love, *Labour and the Money Power, Australian Labour Populism, 1890-1950*, Melbourne University Press, Carlton, 1984.

[12] D.W. Rawson, The Organisation of the Australian Labor Party 1916-1941, PhD thesis, School of Political Science, Criminology and Sociology, Arts, The University of Melbourne, 1954.

Chapter 11: Business Life

[1] Weber's essay was originally a speech at Munich University in 1918 and published in German in 1919. See: Max Weber, 'Politics as a Vocation', in H.H. Gerth and C. Wright Mills, translators and editors, *From Max Weber: Essays in Sociology*, Routledge & Kegan Paul Ltd., London, 1946, pp. 77-128.

[2] What is now known as the Rondavels in *Mpumalanga* province (previously part of the since 1994 defunct Transvaal province of South Africa) are three round mountain tops shaped like the traditional round or oval African homesteads made with local materials called rondavels. In this quote, I changed Ellis' spelling of Rhondarval to Rondavels.

[3] M.H. Ellis, 'Watson – The Forgotten Man', *The Bulletin*, Vol. 84, No. 4305, 18 August 1962, p. 28. In adapting the quote, Tewksbury is spelt correctly, with only one 'e'.

[4] [Report], *The Sydney Mail and New South Wales Advertiser*, 13 April 1910, p. 25. In the quote, I changed Labour to Labor.

[5] The Watson Syndicate. Disappointing Reports, *Sydney Morning Herald*, 2 June 1910, p. 8. Those MPs who were investors are not named in the article.

[6] The Watson Syndicate. Interests Probably Abandoned. Mr Watson Holds All His Shares, *The Sydney Morning Herald*, 4 June 1910, p. 14.

[7] Motoring For Those Who Don't. Melbourne's Rainbow Taxi Cabs. Latest Company to Flaunt a Yellow Sign. What Tewksbury Has Done to Keep Victorians on the Move, *Smith's Weekly*, 17 May 1924, p. 24.

[8] Mrs. J.C. Watson, *Sydney Morning Herald*, 20 July 1921, p. 14.

[9] Widow of Mr. J.C. Watson Dies, *The Sydney Morning Herald*, 4 July 1952, p. 5.

[10] Quietly Married. Mr. J.C. Watson. Motoring Honeymoon, *The Sun* [Sydney], 4 October 1925, p. 2.

[11] M.H. Ellis, 'Watson – The Forgotten Man', *The Bulletin*, Vol. 84, No. 4305, 18 August 1962, p. 31.

[12] Known as Sir Owen, a friend of W.M. Hughes, Cox in March 1920 was foundation president of the National Roads Association (NRA). Apparently, the pressure of other business interests precluded long term engagement. He resigned soon after the NRA was formed, with Watson his successor. Cox was appointed KBE in 1918 and KGBE in 1920. See: Heather Radi, 'Cox,

Sir Edward John Owen (1866-1932)', ADB, National Centre of Biography, ANU, https://adb.anu.edu.au/biography/cox-sir-edward-john-owen-5798/text9839, published first in hardcopy 1981, accessed online 18 November 2023.

[13] Smith's Personalities – No. 53 [J.C. Watson], *Smith's Weekly*, 8 June 1929, p. 12; Broomhall, Loc. Cit., pp. 18f.

[14] Cf. T.C. Barker, 'The International History of Motor Transport', *The Journal of Contemporary History*, Vol. 20, No. 1, 1985, pp. 3-19.

[15] Upton Sinclair, *Oil!*, self-published, Pasadena [California], 1927, p. 1.

[16] Alleged Merger "Conversations" Are Discussed. *The Open Road* [journal of the NRMA], Vol 14, No. 2, 16 January 1936, p. 11.

[17] 'Observer', Men of Sydney. Now Prime Minister of Auto Australia. Mr J.C. Watson, *The Sun* [Sydney], 5 March 1937, p. 10.

[18] Cf. Cheaper Petrol for Members is NRMA's Idea, *The Open Road* [journal of the NRMA], Vol. 7, No. 7, 29 August 1929, p. 1.

[19] Smith's Personalities – No. 53 [J.C. Watson], Loc. Cit., p. 12.

[20] 'Observer', Men of Sydney. Now Prime Minister of Auto Australia. Loc. Cit.

[21] Oil War. If Petrol Price Goes Up. Bruce's Threat. Huge Profits Made in Australia, *The Sun* [Sydney, NSW], 4 August 1926, p. 4.

[22] Over years there were numerous references in the press about Watson and the NRMA's "concerns", "opposition to", "alarm" about petrol taxes, including the potential deleterious impacts on local businesses, the utility of the average family being able to afford a long holiday drive in a car, the regressive impact on lower-income drivers, and so forth. For a few examples: Views of NRMA President, *The Age* [Melbourne, Victoria], 5 August 1926, p.10; New Petrol Tax. Big Knock to Industry. Further Unemployment Feared, *The Armidale Express and New England General Advertiser* [NSW], 14 July 1930, p. 8.

[23] Moves in Petrol Price Changes, *The Sun* [Sydney, NSW], 22 June 1933, p. 17.

[24] Rosemary Broomham, *On the Road: The NRMA's First Seventy-Five Years*, Loc. Cit., p. 64.

[25] Barrie Dyster, 'Walkley, Sir William Gaston (1896-1976)', ADB, National Centre of Biography, ANU, https://adb.anu.edu.au/biography/walkley-sir-william-gaston-11940/text21397, published first in hardcopy 2002, accessed online 24 November 2023.

[26] Cheaper Petrol. New Company's Aim, The Australian Motorists' Petrol Association, *Newcastle Morning Herald and Miners' Advocate*, 18 February, 1936, p. 7.

[27] Cf. Abridged Prospectus. The Australian Motorists Petrol Co. Ltd., *The Open Road* [journal of the NRMA], Vol. 14, No. 5, 27 February 1936, p. 7, & Con-

fidence in the Australian Motorists Petrol Co. Ltd. Demonstrated, *The Open Road* [journal of the NRMA], Vol. 14, No. 9, 23 April 1936, p. 7.

[28] Much of the Ampol story is told in: Colin Simpson, *Show Me a Mountain...*, Loc. Cit.. Watson's role in the formative period of the company is discussed at pp. 10-17.

[29] Noel Sanders, 'Private Faces in Public Spaces: The NRMA, 1920-51', in Helen Wilson, editor, *Australian Communications and the Public Sphere*, Palgrave, London, 1989, p. 208.

[30] Patrol Men, *Good Roads* magazine, NRMA, March 1924. The NRMA's journal *Good Roads* was launched in 1921, changing its name to *The Open Road* in 1927.

[31] 'Guarantors for NRMA Insurance Company, 10 March 1925', Broomham, Loc. Cit., p. 223.

[32] "Printer's Devil" to Prime Minister, *The Daily Telegraph* [Sydney, NSW], 14 January 1928, p. 7.

[33] Old Dog for Hard Road, *Sunday Times* [Sydney, NSW], 15 January 1928, p. 3.

[34] J.C. Watson, Motors and Politics. An Organisation with a Paradoxical Policy, *Evening News* [Sydney, NSW], 12 December 1930, p. 6.

[35] M.H. Ellis, Loc. Cit., p. 28.

Chapter 12: Concluding Observations

[1] David Malouf, *A Spirit of Play. The Making of Australian Consciousness*, [1998 Boyer Lectures broadcast on ABC radio], ABC Books, Sydney 1998, p. 76.

[2] L.F. Fitzhardinge, 'Hughes, William Morris (Billy) (1862-1952)', ADB, National Centre of Biography, ANU, https://adb.anu.edu.au/biography/hughes-william-morris-billy-6761/text11689, published first in hardcopy 1983, accessed online 22 November 2023.

[3] A notice in the newspapers referred to a final rally at the Maccabean Hall for Speaker Hon Daniel Levy MLA, selected National Candidate, supported by Hon. J.C. Watson, ex-Prime Minister: Advertising, *Sydney Morning Herald*, 26 May 1925, p. 16. Levy was a MLA, 1901-1937, and the Speaker in the NSW Parliament, 1919-20, 1920-21, 1921-25, 1927-30 and 1932-37. Controversially, during Labor Premier Dooley's government, Levy's acceptance of the Speakership helped keep that government in office. See: L.E. Fredman, 'Levy, Sir Daniel (1872-1937)', ADB, National Centre of Biography, ANU, https://adb.anu.edu.au/biography/levy-sir-daniel-7181/text12411, published first in hardcopy 1986, accessed online 22 November 2023.

[4] Personal, *Sydney Morning Herald*, 1 November 1929, p. 12.

5 Seen From the Window, *The Australian Worker* [Sydney, NSW], 13 November 1929, p. 1.

6 Chamber of Manufactures, *Sydney Morning Herald*, 3 December 1929, p. 6.

7 John Robertson, *J.H. Scullin*, University of Western Australia Press, Nedlands, 1974.

8 Information about Watson as a Trustee of the SCG was supplied by Rodney Cavalier, a former Trustee, who is writing an official history of Trustees of the SCG with sports historian Geoff Armstrong. Rodney forwarded to me references to Watson in the SCG Minutes.

9 "He played golf until a few months before his death" and was a past president of the Woollahra Golf Club, and a member of the Australian Golf Club: First Labor P.M. Dead, *Daily Mirror* [Sydney, NSW], 18 November 1941, p. 5.

10 The Two Million, *The Daily Telegraph*, 26 March 1937, p. 8.

11 Email, Rodney Cavalier to Michael Easson, 22 November 2023.

12 Geoff Armstrong and Rodney Cavalier, 'Trustees of the SCG and the Great War and the Flu Pandemic that Followed', *Southern Highlands Newsletter*, No. 238, May-June 2020, p. 59.

13 Email, Rodney Cavalier to Michael Easson, 22 November 2023.

14 Geoffrey Bolton, 'How Uneasy Lies the Head? The Health of Australian Prime Ministers', *Health and History*, Vo. 1, No. 2/3, 1999, p. 177.

15 Letter: Arthur Griffith to Mrs A. Watson, 21 November 1941, J.C. Watson Papers, NLA MS 451/1/201.

16 English-born Ernest Henry Farrar (1879-1952), saddler, union leader, and politician, was a member of the ALP central executive 1908-1916, vice-president 1909, 1911, 1915-1916, president 1912-1913, expelled from ALP on conscription issue, thereafter a Nationalist and UAP politician, and MLC for forty years, 1912 to his death in 1952. See: former members of the Parliament of New South Wales, retrieved 8 November 2023.

17 Mark Lyons, 'Gardiner, Albert (Jupp) (1867-1952)', ADB, National Centre of Biography, ANU, https://adb.anu.edu.au/biography/gardiner-albert-jupp-6275/text10815, published first in hardcopy 1981, accessed online 26 January 2024.

18 State Funeral, *Sydney Morning Herald*, 21 November 1941, p. 5; Funeral of Former PM, *Daily Telegraph* [Sydney, NSW], 21 November 1941, p. 5.

19 M.H. Ellis, 'Watson – The Forgotten Man', Loc. Cit., p. 31.

20 At the funeral in London of Sir George Reid (1845-1918), the first former Australian Prime Minister to die, the pallbearers included the then Prime Minister, W.M. Hughes and former Prime Minister Sir Joseph Cook (who, fortuitously, were both in England), former Prime Minister Andrew Fisher,

the then Australian High Commissioner; and others from the UK: Sir George Reid's Funeral, *Sydney Morning Herald*, 18 September 1918, p. 11. At the funeral of Alfred Deakin (1856-1919), the pallbearers included the Prime Minister, W.M. Hughes, the leader of the Federal Opposition Frank Tudor, the Victorian Premier (Mr. Lawson), the Chief Justice (Sir William Irvine), Sir Edmund Barton, the Lord Mayor (Alderman Cabena), and several of Deakin's friends: At Deakin's Funeral, *The Age* [Melbourne, Victoria], 9 October 1919, p. 7. The pallbearers of former PM and Chief Justice Edmund Barton (1849-1920) were the Federal Chief Justice (Mr. Justice Knox), the Chief Justice of NSW (Sir Wm. Cullen), the Speaker of the House of Representatives (Mr. W. Elliot Johnson), Mr. Justice Rich, the Minister for Trade and Customs (Mr. Massy Greene) representing the Prime Minister, the Premier of NSW, Mr. Holman, and the Minister for Health, Mr. David Storey: Impressive Scenes. Primate's Panegyric, *Sydney Morning Herald*, 10 January 1920, p. 13. As with Sir George Reid, Andrew Fisher (1862-1928) died and was buried in the UK. But no Australian political leaders were reported as pallbearers, due to the impracticality of travelling quickly to London in those days: Last Tribute. Mr Andrew Fisher, *The Brisbane Courier*, 29 October 1928, p. 13. The pallbearers of the fifth Prime Minister to die, the first in office, Joseph Lyons (1879-1939) were the Prime Minister, Sir Earle Page, the Minister for External Affairs, Mr. Hughes, the Federal Treasurer, Mr. Casey, the Leader of the Opposition, Mr Curtin, the Labor Premier of Tasmania, Mr. Ogilvie, the Leader of the Tasmanian Opposition, Mr. Baker, and several friends of the late Prime Minister: Mr Lyons' Funeral, *Courier-Mail* [Brisbane, Queensland], 14 April 1939, p. 3. Watson was the sixth former Australian Prime Minister to die.

[21] With Curtin's funeral in Perth, the pallbearers included the Acting Prime Minister, Mr F.M. Forde, Federal Opposition Leader Mr R.G. Menzies, and others, including local political leaders. Chifley was too grief-stricken to attend: The State Funeral of Mr John Curtin, *The West Australian* [Perth], 9 July 1945, p. 6. With Sir Joseph Cook's funeral in 1947, the pallbearers included the former PM, Mr W.M. Hughes, the Minister for Supply and Shipping, Senator Ashley, the NSW Labor Premier, Mr. McGirr, Tom Sheehan, MHR, representing the Labor Opposition, and others: Funeral of Sir J. Cook, *Daily Mirror* [Sydney, NSW], 1 August 1947, p. 2. At Chifley's funeral, there was cross-party representation with pallbearers Prime Minister Menzies, the Acting Opposition Leader Dr Evatt, the Deputy Prime Minister, Sir Arthur Fadden, the Leader of the Government in the Senate, Senator O'Sullivan, the Leader of the Opposition in the Senate, Senator McKenna, the President of the Senate, Senator Mattner, and the Speaker of the House of Representatives, Mr. Cameron: Body of J.B. Chifley to Lie in State. Funeral in Bathurst, *The Canberra Times*, 15 June 1951, p. 1.

[22] Al Grassby and Silvia Ordonez, *The Man Time Forgot. Loc. Cit.*, p. 164.

[23] J.C. Watson, [typed manuscript] The Labor Movement, n.d., circa 1914, J.C. Watson Papers, NLA MS 451/2/1, pp. 1-2.

[24] J.C. Watson, [typed manuscript], [under sub-heading 'Conclusion'] The Labor Movement, Ibid, p. 16.

INDEX

1916 ALP conscription split, 11, 95ff, 134
Alexandria Spinning Mills, 117
Allen, Woody, 71
ALP Solidarity Conference, 34, 133
Ampol, 113, 125ff
Anstey, Frank, 115
anti-Chinese, 39, 40
anti-socialist, 46, 57
Archduke Franz Ferdinand, 95
Arkins, James, 105
Ashford, William, 105
Asquith, H.H., 92
Australian Constitution, 5, 15, 20
Australian Imperial Force, 96, 112, 137
Australian Industries Protection League, 138
Australian National Defence League, 88
Australian Natives Association, 56
Australian Navy, 93
Australian Shipping Line, 96
Australian Town and Country Journal, 54
AWU, 98, 106

Bagnall, William, 105
Bailey, Jack, 114
Ballaarat electorate, 66
Bamford, Frederick, 45
Barber, Frank, 78. 80
Barrett, John, 45

Barton, Edmund, 43, 44, 56
Batchelor, Lee, 45, 53, 55, 60
Bavin, Thomas, 129
Beazley, Kim E., 8, 10, 63, 107
Beeby, George, 78
Belich, James, 31
Bentham, Jeremy, 78
Bernstein, Eduard, 79, 85
Bilson, John, 78
Black, George, 76, 82, 85, 97, 106
Borden, Robert, 92
Bounty Regulation Migrants, 16
Brady, Edwin James, 76
Brennan, Peter Joseph, 75
British Association for the Advancement of Science, 6
British Australian, 5, 135
British Royal Naval Reserve, 89
Broomham, Rosemary, 126
Brown, Thomas, 45
Bruce, Stanley Melbourne, 138
Burgess, George, 105

Canberra, 71
Cardinal Moran, 66, 68
Carruthers, Joseph, 118
Catholic Church of Matriz, 20
Catholic Young Mens' Association, 34
Catts, James, 65, 90, 97, 115, 138
Cavalier, Rodney, 139
Cave Valley, 22

Central Powers, 111
Chifley, Ben, 140
Childe, Vere Gordon, 113
Christian Socialism, 42, 80
Christianity, 40
Citizens' Defence Force, 92
Civilising Capitalism, 81
Clark, Manning, 107
Clune, David, xi
Commonwealth Bank, 9
Commonwealth Liberal Party, 74
Communism, 66
compulsory arbitration, 7, 48
Conciliation and Arbitration Act, 64
Conciliation and Arbitration Bill, 53, 63
Cook, Joseph, 34, 37, 108, 140
Cox, Owen, 119
Crawford, Thomas, 105
Crick, Bernard, 48
Curtin, John, 13, 116, 140
Cyclopedia of New Zealand, 24

Dancey, George Henry, 44
David, Edgeworth, 98
Davis, Thomas Martin, 77
Dawson, Anderson, 45, 53, 56
de Largie, Hugh, 95
Deakin, Alfred, 7, 9, 10, 43, 44, 57-59, 63, 64, 70, 71, 89
Dornbusch's Law, 11, 111
Dowlan, Antonia Mary Gladys, ix, 19, 40, 119, See Mrs Watson
Doyle, Jack, 102
Dunn, Jacqueline, 6, 19, 119

Dyster, Barrie, 127
Edden, Arthur, 105
Eight-Hour Demonstration, 33
Ellis, M.H., 29, 32, 76, 119, 120, 140
Employers' Liability Act, 75
Ethics of Labor Legislation, 78
Evans, Percy Charles, 105, 114
Evatt, H.V., 114

Farrar, Ernie, 140
Federation, 40
Ferguson, W.J., 40
Findley, Ted, 50, 90
First conscription referendum result, 104
Fisher, Andrew, 68, 71, 95, 96, 135, 140
Fitzgerald, Jack, 76, 83, 97
Fitzhardinge, L.F., 34, 64, 137
Ford Model T, 127
Forrest, John, 69, 108
Fowler, James, 45, 67
Free Trade, 9, 10, 35, 57
Freudenberg, Graham, 64
Fusion, 66, 73

Gardiner, Albert, 140
Gardiner, Arthur, 105
George, Henry, 39
German Social Democrats, 85
Gold Rush, 22, 39, 40
Governor Carrington, 10, 32
Grace, Damian, xi
Grant, Jack, 65. 66
Grassby and Ordonez, 5, 6, 22

Great Potato Famine, 16
Griffith, Arthur, 77, 97, 104, 105, 139, 140

H.W. Hughes Pty Ltd., 118
Hagan, Jim, 34, 113
Hall, David, 105, 140
Harding, Catherine, xi
Harvester Judgement, 9
Heagney, Patrick, 66
Higgins, Henry Bournes, 9, 53, 55, 64
Higgs, William, 45
High Court of Australia, 9, 24, 64
Holder, Frederick, 61
Hollis, Robert, 105
Holman, William, 55, 78, 90, 97, 104, 113, 139
"Hop", xii
Hourn, W.A., 36
Hoyle, Henry, 105
Hughes, Fred William, 119, 124
Hughes, William Morris, 78, 87, 89, 96, 101-4, 107, 112, 113, 135, 137, 140
Hutchison, George, 126

Imperial Parliamentary Association, 92
Imperial War Office, 136
Industrial Vigilance Council, 106
Isaacs, Isaac, 9, 14, 64

John Oxley Library, 49
Jones, George, 29

Kelly, Andrew Joseph, 76
Kingston, Charles, 56

La Joven Julia, 18
La Nauze, John, 25, 43
Labor Caucus, 43, 107
Labor Conference of 1905, 66ff
Labor Council of NSW, 98
Labor's Objective, 67
Laborism, 43, 50
Lambing Flat. *See* Young
Lamond, Hector, 66, 98, 102, 104, 109
Lane, Antonia. *See* Mrs Watson, *See* Mrs Watson
Lane, William, 32, 77
Lang, Jack, 8, 116, 138
Leader newspaper, 37
Levy, Daniel, 138
Lewis, George, 98
Liberalism, 9, 14, 46, 54
Lindsay, Lionel, 51
Lloyd's of London, 129
Lord Northcote, 53, 63
Lord, James, 18
Low, Ada, 40, 71, 72, 119
Lycidas, 63
Lyne, William, 7, 87
Lyons, Joe, 138
MacDonald, Charles, 43, 45
Macdonell House, 106
Macdonell, Donald, 66
Macintyre, Stuart, 8
Mahon, Hugh, 45, 47, 53, 56, 59, 64
Massey, William, 92

Masters and Servants Act, 75
McGowen, James, 85, 105
McGregor, Gregor, 56
McKell, William, 8, 9, 13, 18, 102, 116, 140
McLean, Allan, 64
McMullin, Ross, 11, 60
Meagher, Dick, 97, 99, 105
Meaney, Neville, 87, 97
Mercer, James, 105
Métin, Albert, 82
Milton, John, 63
Minchin, Ellen, 15
Minchin, Martha. See Martha Watson, 19
Minchin, William, 16, 17
Mitchell, James, 23, 26, 28
Molesworth, James, 77
Mormon Church, 20
Morrish, James, 105
Mrs Watson, 75
Mrs. Ada Watson. See Low, Ada

Nairn, Bede, xi, 13, 81
National Archives, 62
National Labor Party, 108, 136
National Portrait Gallery, 44
National Roads and Motorists Association, 3, 8, 113, 120ff
National Roads Association, 121
Nationalist Party, 109, 137
navvying, 22
New Australia, 35, 77
New Zealand Land League, 22
Newcastle Morning Herald, 48

Nicholson, John, 105
North Otago Times, 22
Northern Territory, 87

O'Callaghan, Arthur, 126
O'Connor, R.E., 39
O'Hara, Lawrence, 106
O'Keefe, David, 45
O'Malley, King, 5, 69, 90, 92
Oamaru, 25-29
Oamaru Mail, 22, 24, 26, 27, 30
Old Bailey, 17
Otago Province, 10ff

Page, Jim, 45
Paraguay, 32, 77
Parkes, Henry, 76
Pearce, George, 45, 47, 69, 73, 135
Perks, Murray, 93, 100
Pix, 53
Plumbers' Union, 76
Political Labor League, 34, 101
Pope Leo XIII, 66
Poynton, Alec, 50
Protectionist, 9, 10, 37, 56, 64
Prussian militarism, 15

Rae, Arthur, 98
Reid, George Houston, 7, 10, 43, 57, 59, 63, 89
Rerum Novarum, 66
Riley, Edward, 66
Ronald, James, 45
Round Table, 97
Royal Automobile Club of Australia, 122

Sawer, Geoffrey, 9, 10, 14, 75
Scobie, Robert, 66, 105
Scullin, James, 9, 14, 69, 138
Settler Australia, 31
Sinclair, Upton, 122, 126, 127
Skinner, Martha Ellen. *See* Minchin, Martha, 19
Smeaton, Tom, 68
Snowden, Philip, 92
South Africa, 72, 73, 118
Spence, William Guthrie, 45, 66, 101
State Socialism, 71
Stewart, James, 45
Storey, John, 113
Support in Return for Concessions, 82
Surveyor General of Tasmania, 18
Sydney Cricket Ground Trust, 138

Tanck, Johan Christian, 5, 18
Tewksbury, William, 72, 118, 130
The Australasian, 47
The Call. *See* Australian National Defence League
The Globe, 32
The Labor pledge, 34
Second conscription referendum result, 112
The Star, 32
The Things That Are, 85
The Tocsin, 79
Thomas, Josiah, 46, 47
Thompson, Claude, 98
Three Elevens, 56

Timaru Herald, 24
Trade Union Act, 76
Trades and Labour Council, 31, 37, 75, 79
Transvaal, 72, 118
Tudor, Frank, 113, 114
Turner, George, 61
Turner, Ken, 34, 113

Unitarian Church, 40-43, 80
United Australia Party, 8, 140
Universal Service League, 97, 98
Utopia, 32

Valparaiso, Chile, 5, 10, 19, 22
Vincent, Arthur James, 61

Waipori, 22
Walkley, George, 126
Walters, Rev. George, 42
Watkins, David, 45
Watson, Catherine, xi, 17, 21
Watson, George Thomas, 5, 17, 21
Weber, Max, 12, 84, 118
West Sydney, 34, 76, 83
West, John, 34, 77
Weston, 22
Whitehall, 53, 63
Williams, Roy, 40
Workingman's Paradise, 78
World War I, 10, 95-116

Yellow Cabs, 130
Young, 35, 37-39, 126

www.ingramcontent.com/pod-product-compliance
Lightning Source LLC
Chambersburg PA
CBHW070357240426
43671CB00013BA/2536